HOW TO RAISE A GOOD KID
A Guide to Growing Up for Parents & Children

Starbuck O'Dwyer is a graduate of Princeton, Oxford and Cornell. His novel, *Red Meat Cures Cancer* (Random House/Vintage), was a featured selection of the 2007 One Book One Vancouver reading program and won two national writing awards for humor. Starbuck's work has appeared in numerous publications and has been described as "comic genius" by *Kirkus Reviews*. Visit his website at www.starbuckodwyer.com.

Also by Starbuck O'Dwyer

Red Meat Cures Cancer
Goliath Gets Up

HOW TO RAISE A GOOD KID
A Guide to Growing Up for Parents & Children

STARBUCK O'DWYER

GCP
GREEN CHAIR PUBLISHING — NEW YORK

Copyright © 2009 by Starbuck O'Dwyer

GCP
GREEN CHAIR PUBLISHING NEW YORK

ISBN 13: 978-0615485324
ISBN 10: 0615485324

All rights reserved under International and Pan-American Copyright Conventions. No part of this book may be reproduced or transmitted in any form or by any means, electronic or mechanical, including but not limited to photocopying, electronic mail, recording or by any information storage or retrieval system, without permission in writing from the copyright holder. Names, characters, places and incidents either are the product of the author's imagination or are used fictitiously, and any resemblance to any actual persons, living or dead, events or locales is entirely coincidental. Trademarks and service names have been used throughout this book and are owned by their respective trademark holders. Rather than insert a trademark notation at each occurrence of the name, the publisher states that all such trademarks are used in an editorial manner without any intent to infringe upon the trademark.

For K, R and V, with all my love

Contents

1	The Importance of Enthusiasm	1
2	The Value of Fathers	9
3	Loyalty	15
4	Prejudice	23
5	Self-Expression	29
6	How to Handle a Bully	35
7	Popularity	41
8	Courage	47
9	First Crushes	55
10	Hard Work	63
11	Persistence	69
12	Self-Determination	77
13	Necessary Rites of Passage	85
14	The Meaning of Tradition	91
15	Adapting to Change	97
16	Beauty	105
17	Honesty	111
18	Patriotism	119
19	Punishment	129
20	Faith	135
21	Resiliency	139
22	The Wisdom of Mothers	145
23	Love and Marriage	153

1
The Importance of Enthusiasm

Forward Ho

In the spring of 1976, my father had an idea. In celebration of our country's Bicentennial, he would take our whole family cross country on a summer camping expedition. It was a bold stroke given that all of us, including him, hated camping. But he was determined to show us the beauty of our great nation and equally committed to doing so on a budget. The way he saw it: why pay for a safe, comfortable hotel room when you can sleep outside at a state park next to dangerous strangers for free.

Nobody has ever mistaken my father for a consensus builder. A product of the patriarchal 1950's, he believes that true leaders refuse to be hindered by the pesky input of others, especially family members. Accordingly, he announced our trip the way he announced all major decisions affecting us; at the dinner table when my mother's defenses were down. He knew she would be too exhausted after teaching all day to object to a family vacation, even one involving bug spray and Sterno, while serving up steaming mounds of beef stroganoff to her brood.

Having learned from years of experience that my father was an irresistible force when it came to his own ideas, my mother immediately set about assessing the damage.

"Will we go for two weeks, honey?" she asked gingerly; keenly aware of my father's tendency to overdo.

"I'm thinking six," he said.

"Six weeks?" she asked, choking on her stroganoff.

As the owner of his own business, my father could take lengthy vacations.

"Six maybe seven," my father said. "You can't see anything in two weeks."

"Not in a tent, though, right?" my mother asked; the fear in her voice rising.

"No, not a tent," he said.

"Oh, thank God," she said.

"Two tents. One for us and one for the kids."

With skill and luck, my mother could sometimes move my father and his ideas in a better direction. In this case, by repeatedly reminding him of the 13 weeks they spent in a tent as a newly married couple and her inability to have a bowel movement during that entire period, she was able to convince him that a recreational vehicle with indoor plumbing was in order. Shortly thereafter, he took me to the RV dealership to explore rental options.

On the lot, we were met by Eddie, a salesman with a plaid jacket and a plastic smile, who immediately steered us to a vehicle best described as a battleship on wheels.

"Seems awful big," my father said. "What kind of gas mileage does it get?"

"About four miles a gallon, but if you want to see the country in style this summer, this is the rig I recommend. Climb aboard El Conquistador, gentleman," Eddie said, opening the door for us.

"Spacious," my father said as we moved into its cabin.

"Oh, yeah, real spacious and loaded, too. You've got your master bedroom, your kitchen, your game room, your hi-fi stereo. This baby's even bullet-proof," Eddie crowed.

"Really?" my father asked.

"That's what my manager says," Eddie replied.

"Do you think we'll get shot at during the trip, Dad?" I asked warily.

"Probably not," he said. "But it's a good feature to have just in case."

Unfortunately, as soon as Eddie shared the rental price, my father abandoned the dream of the RV and asked to see an Airstream trailer; an elongated silver cocoon he could hitch to our station wagon.

"These are nice," my father said, running his hand along the Airstream's sleek surface.

"Sure, no doubt," Eddie said. "You're not gonna have all your features as you would with El Conquistador, but the Airstream will get you from A to B."

"That's the goal," my father said. "What's it rent for?" he asked, after we'd toured the interior.

Eddie's answer was similarly unsatisfactory and we soon moved as a group to the farthest end of the lot to find something that was, "better than a tent, but not as good as an Airstream," as my father put it. This left us in the pop-up camper category.

All the pop-up campers looked the same; like oversized ice cream sandwiches when closed and like Jiffy Pop bags when open. They were unsightly to say the least, but the price was right and Eddie assured my father that set up was a breeze.

"Just pop the top when you get to the campsite and, 42 quick steps later, you're ready to bunk down for the night."

And with that, a deal was made. My father loved to drive a hard bargain and he clearly felt good as he hitched our new camper to the car. Driving home, however, I inadvertently soured his self-congratulatory mood.

"Do you think Mom will care that there's no bathroom?" I asked.

"Let's not mention that yet," he said. "We'll save some surprises for the road."

The day of the trip arrived and it was impossible not to get caught up in my father's enthusiasm.

"Forward Hohhh!" He yelled as we pulled out of our circular driveway; a guttural call to action he would soon have all of us shouting in unison each time the car left its station. He was a master at making you believe you were having fun whether you were or not.

"Isn't this great?" he asked excitedly, as we rolled through Erie, Pennsylvania. "This is the same route that Lewis and Clark traveled."

"No, it's not, Dad," my sister said.

"Well, it's similar," he replied.

He was also skilled at convincing you each sight you saw was significant; a true feat considering there was nothing to see between Western New York and Colorado besides Mount Rushmore. He exuded a brand of American optimism; a belief that something better was just around the next corner. And it was futile to resist.

"Kids, what you see before you are the most historic sand dunes in the country," my father said, as we stood in the middle of Indiana Dunes National Park.

"What's so historic about them?" I asked.

"Aren't they magnificent?" he asked, ignoring my question completely. "Wait'll you see what's ahead."

On the road, despite the lack of a DVD player or hand held devices of any kind, my parents tried to keep my sister and me busy with a series of diversions. There were Mad Libs and crossword puzzles, quizzes on state capitols and presidents, and, of course, sing-alongs. There were also frequent sibling fights that broke out in the backseat as we got on each other's nerves and bounced around like errant pinballs, untethered by seatbelts.

Nevertheless, cruising along the highway and crossing state borders, I felt a true sense of adventure for the first time in my life and it was exhilarating. Every evening, I helped my father set up the camper and start a pit-fire, and ate char-grilled food with my family on tin plates. Drifting off to sleep, I listened nervously to the sound of animals in the woods and accepted my mother's assurances that no bears lived in the area. Safely ensconced behind the locked screen door of our temporary home, I was becoming an avid outdoorsman.

Inevitably, however, as the days and hours of car travel dragged on and the sun beat down through the windows, I grew restless and began to question the point of the whole exercise. My father had guaranteed us sights that would leave us in awe and wonder, and I was starting to think he had vastly over-promised. Traveling through Illinois, Iowa and Nebraska, I kept waiting to be bowled over, but was met with mile after mile of brown, flat land.

Then, suddenly, just when I thought I'd been bamboozled, along came the Rocky Mountains, emerging on the horizon like the City of Oz. Moving closer and closer, I was transfixed by their growing immensity. I'd never seen anything like them.

"Wow. Are we going right into the mountains?" I asked, my enthusiasm having returned.

"Straight into the belly of the beast," my father said. "We'll climb to almost 13,000 feet above sea level."

"Cool," I said, my excitement evident.

"Forward, hohhh!" we shouted.

Rocky Mountain National Park did not disappoint. Neither did Yellowstone, Bryce, Zion or the Grand Canyon; each one spectacular in its own way. Over the next two weeks, as we camped in these five places, I became a convert to my father's idea and vision. Seeing these places of natural beauty was important, inspiring and historically significant. He was right all along and whatever complaining I'd been doing about long drives and a hot car immediately stopped. As we left the Grand Canyon, I was ready for more.

"So what's next, Dad? Yosemite? Maybe Redwoods?" I asked, having hijacked the guide book my parents were using. "I've always heard good things about Glacier."

"We're not going to any more national parks," my father said.

"We're not?" I asked. "Where are we going?"

"Vegas," my father said.

"Vegas?" I asked.

When my father pulled our Ford Country Squire

How to Raise a Good Kid

station wagon into the fountain-clad driveway of Caesar's Palace and handed his keys to the valet, he looked happier than I'd ever seen him. What I hadn't realized was that the rigors of the outdoors had finally caught up with my parents. My father was sick and tired of assembling the pop-up camper and my mother hadn't had a bowel movement in nearly a month. They were ready for a real shower, a king-sized bed and a hot meal served on something other than industrial-strength aluminum. So just like that, with one hotel reservation, our family's great flirtation with nature was over.

Amazingly, my sister and I adjusted quickly to hotel life and were soon ordering room service like pros, watching Blazing Saddles on cable TV and begging to play the nickel slots. Along with my parents, we swam and sunbathed by an enormous pool, and grew accustomed to the good life, however brief.

After our stint at Caesar's, we never stayed in the pop-up camper again. The route home, which took us through New Mexico, Texas, Oklahoma, Arkansas and Tennessee, before leading northward to New York, was spent in state capitols like Albuquerque and Little Rock, where we took in the tourist attractions and slept at Holiday Inns.

Although he'd blown the trip budget with motel charges and driven past a number of national monuments and parks that we'd originally planned to visit, my father was philosophical about his choices; reminding all of us that we'd saved money by renting a pop-up camper and that we'd seen all the truly worthwhile sights. Still, as our leader, he wondered whether he'd done the right thing for his wife and his children and whether or not the trip had met the high expectations he set at the beginning. As we arrived home, he revealed himself by asking the one question that could resolve these things in his mind.

"Good family trip, don't you think?" he asked, parking in our driveway and turning his head to face us; his American optimism wavering for just the briefest of seconds.

For once, the man who never solicited our opinions was doing just that.

"Yeah, Dad. It was," I said. "I loved the sand dunes."

"Good trip, Dad," my sister replied.

"It's been a wonderful trip, honey," my mother said.

"Of course it was," he said, reverting to form. "I told you guys."

After unpacking, my father and I climbed back into our station wagon to return the pop-up camper.

"Do you want to do the honors?" he asked me as he put the car in drive.

"Sure," I said, smiling at him. "Forward hohhh!"

2
The Value of Fathers

Pals Forever

Around age six, I began to see kids in Cub Scout uniforms everywhere. Their blue shirts and baseball caps appeared harmless enough but the golden handkerchief tied around their necks horrified me. Wearing a tie was the ultimate expression of conformity and I wanted no part of it. So, naturally, I recoiled when my parents asked if I wanted to join a local troop.

Not long after I said no, however, the chance to be part of a different group arose. Keenly aware of my contrarian spirit, my parents took careful steps to avoid scaring me off the opportunity. They described Indian Guides as a loosely banded faction of anarchists; explaining that it was more akin to a street gang than a youth organization. "If you don't like it, we'll quit," my father said, and with that assurance I was sold.

In reality, Indian Guides was a program sponsored by the YMCA with the purpose of promoting close relationships between fathers and sons. Originated in 1926 by Harold Keltner, a St. Louis Y director, it was inspired by the teachings of an Ojibway Indian named Joe Friday who spoke about the important role fathers play helping boys become men in Indian culture through hunting, fishing and tracking as well as spiritual and moral development. Hoping to replicate this dynamic in suburban America, Mr. Keltner turned alchemist; mixing traditional Indian activities and symbols with modern life to create Indian Guides.

Our first meeting, like most that would follow, was held in a neighbor's garage at night in the middle of winter. Homes in our neighborhood were small and none of the mothers were foolish enough to believe anything good could come from allowing ten men and their rambunctious sons, soon-to-be wearing war paint, into her living room. This was wise policy given that all gatherings commenced with the noisy beating of a ceremonial drum; an event that usually lasted at least 15 minutes as each kid took his turn.

The next order of business at the first meeting was selecting our Indian names. Creativity must have been frowned upon back then because nobody came up with anything cool like Dances with Wolves or Farts like a Pro. Instead it was all big and little as in Big Bear — Little Bear, Big Hawk — Little Hawk and so on. Unfortunately, by the time my father and I got to choose, everything formidable or ferocious was taken and we ended up as Big Cloud — Little Cloud. Seeing the disappointment on my face, my father said we'd have the last laugh when the time came for a rain dance, but I wasn't buying it.

Without an oath to recite or merit badges to pursue, the fathers seemed largely at a loss regarding what to do with us following the banging of the drum and the selection of names. Hunting and fishing were out given the setting and tracking was difficult unless you were tracking a 1973 Chevy Nova; which by now had been moved out of the garage and was sitting in the driveway. Nobody felt like going outside anyway since it was 45 degrees below zero, a typical temperature in Rochester, New York where we lived.

Mostly we ate and drank; activities everyone could agree upon. Despite being inside a sealed garage, host fathers never hesitated to light up their Weber grills. First of all, it was always freezing and the garages were universally unheated. Second, when the smoke from the charcoal got so bad that everyone was choking, the Littles, as the boys were known, would take turns manually opening the garage door to let it out; thereby creating an activity for the group.

We didn't have uniforms but we each made vests, cut from tan cloth with fringe around the perimeter, which we coupled with headbands and feathers to create a look similar to Peter Fonda's in Easy Rider. Then we added war paint to our faces; transforming ourselves into the living embodiment of all dressed up with nowhere to go as we sat in the garage eating hot dogs and hamburgers and breathing in fumes from the lighter fluid being doused on the briquettes.

As the weeks went on, arts and crafts began to dominate the agenda. Soon, an organization meant to principally involve the great outdoors was largely devoted to sand painting, Popsicle stick architecture and gluing small rocks to twigs. Admittedly, this was the kind of undemanding and unstructured dynamic I'd been promised, but even I was surprised at what seemed like a complete absence of any substance. We didn't learn how to tie knots, start fires or administer CPR. We didn't help little old ladies cross the street or sell cookies for charity. Indian Guides was turning out to be the true antithesis of Cub Scouts and, even though I loved every minute of it, I felt a bit conflicted. Wasn't there supposed to be a purpose to all this?

When Rochester's snowfall finally cleared (sometime around June 1st), our tribe, dubbed the Tuscaroras by my father, made its one and only foray into the woods with a four-day trip to Camp Cory, a YMCA camp located on Keuka Lake an hour away by car. Once there, we came close to achieving what I imagined to be the Indian Guides ideal as we swam, canoed and tried to learn archery without killing each other in the process. At night, we sat around the campfire, roasted marshmallows and sang the songs one sings on such occasions before retiring to cabins with our dads. It was a perfect trip and, as it turned out, it was my last.

I only spent one year in Indian Guides. We moved away and I never saw any of Bigs or the Littles again. And as time went by, I forgot all about them and the fact I'd ever been a part of the program until I was rooting around in my parents' attic one day as a new father and came across a box of childhood clothing my mother had kept. Inside, beneath tee-shirts and Toughskins my mom couldn't bear to part with, was my Indian Guides vest, still adorned with the patch provided by the YMCA that she'd sewn on for me.

Looking at the vest, I felt my memories of the experience coming back to me. The patch was circular with the words "INDIAN" and "GUIDES" spread across the top and bottom of its curvature. In the center was an arrowhead with the acronym "YMCA" embedded on it. And had that been all, I may never have remembered nor fully grasped the importance of what transpired so many years before. But, to my good fortune, when I looked a bit closer there was something more on the patch.

Just above the arrowhead, blended into the background, were the words "Father and Son" and below it "Pals Forever" — the official motto of Indian Guides. I paused and thought more about my days as Little Cloud and what this chapter in my life had been all about. It didn't matter that our meetings were held in neighborhood garages. It didn't matter that all we did was eat, drink and create the world's worst arts and crafts. It didn't even matter that none of us learned to hunt, fish or trap anything other than the mouse that once interrupted a meeting at Jeff Brasser's house. None of that was important.

Indian Guides had one sole purpose: fostering close relationships between fathers and sons that would last a lifetime. The founder may have had loftier hopes in terms of the incorporation of Indian-themed activities and culture into the day-to-day functioning of the organization, but I believe he would have been pleased by the incredible tally of hours spent together by fathers and sons because of him and the resulting impact. Sure, the motto was hokey, but did the program work? As for me, it put into motion a pattern of regularly doing things with my dad that made me believe he liked spending time with me as much as I liked spending time with him. And, years later, when I decided to get married, my father was the person I wanted standing next to me as my best man. Pals forever? Absolutely.

3
Loyalty

Blankie

Pacifiers held no appeal for me as a kid and my thumb rarely made it anywhere near my mouth. Instead, all my loyalties lay with my blanket, Blankie. I suppose I could have named him something more original like Ed or Charlie or Mudflap, but to me only one name truly fit. Placed in my crib shortly after birth, Blankie was a pale yellow piece of thick cotton that became a very close friend of mine and a big part of my childhood.

Blankie was a good listener and never rambled on with big, dumb stories like other people. He was also very cool, especially on hot summer nights when I used him as a pillow; contentedly laying my head down before drifting off to dreams of glory. Blankie was incredibly sturdy. Unlike some dainty blankets I'd seen, Blankie had the consistency of a day-old bagel and was perfect for chewing on. When one corner became soaked with saliva, I moved on to the next; twisting it up and jamming it into my craw — after which I would happily suck like a boy with a straw in an extra-thick milkshake.

Blankie loved to play and brought impressive utility to any game. He could be an ocean, a tent and a mountain all in the course of a single afternoon. He was also remarkably agreeable, something I truly appreciated having encountered my share of difficult playmates. Whatever I wanted to do was okay with him and no matter how late it got, he was never too tired to start something new. Best of all, he had a wide-open calendar so scheduling things with him was a breeze.

As time went on, Blankie and I remained the best of pals — something I never wanted to change. I saw us a lot like Linus and his blanket. Year after year, they met their challenges together whether it was helping Charlie Brown put on the Christmas pageant or battling doubters of The Great Pumpkin. They were a united team with unquestioning devotion to each other and we were the same way.

Occasionally, someone would question Linus's need for a blanket, but he was always able to shoo them away by demonstrating how useful his blanket could be. When faced with the same question myself, I tried Linus's approach but found little success.

It started when I reached kindergarten and was told that blankets weren't allowed in school. I didn't understand this policy (neither did Blankie) but after much protest, I relented and broke the bad news to him. To his credit, he took it well and was always waiting for me when

I got home; ready to pick back up wherever we'd left off. I made some new friends at school, but none like Blankie.

Unfortunately, with time, I would learn there were lots of places where Blankie's presence was discouraged; everywhere from church and birthday parties to little league baseball tryouts and swimming lessons. It turned out that the world was an inhospitable place for a boy and his blanket and I began to hear the whispers that perhaps I was too old to have one. Still, as the pressure to abandon him mounted, I persisted. I'd take him with me every chance I could, enduring the ridicule and stares that accompanied trips to the grocery store, the public library and occasional weddings and funerals; proudly standing by Blankie whatever the cost.

Eventually, everything came to a head when I was eleven and my father threatened to ship me off to the Army (at least that's how I heard it at first).

"Would you like to see the U.S. Military Academy at West Point?" he asked.

"Are you shipping me off to the Army?" I asked.

"No," he said. "Why would you think that?"

"I'll do better in school," I said. "I swear."

"I'm not shipping you anywhere," my father said.

"Is this about Blankie?"

"No. It's not about Blankie."

"Are you sending me away to school?" I asked.

"No. I just thought you'd like to see West Point's campus and maybe take in a football game."

As a member of the Army reserves, my father had a series of meetings at the academy and had arranged for me to tag along.

"So you promise you won't leave me there?"

"I promise," he said.

After agreeing to go, albeit somewhat reluctantly, I packed my suitcase; carefully folding Blankie and laying him gently between my underwear and socks. He always traveled with me so this was no surprise to him. I figured he'd like to see West Point, too. Plus, he was a huge football fan.

My father wanted this trip to make a big impression on me. He believed I was destined for great things and as we drove toward West Point, he explained to me that many of our country's legendary leaders were graduates of the academy. He said there was a tradition of excellence and that men like Douglas MacArthur, George S. Patton, Jr. and Dwight Eisenhower, among many others, spent four years there sharpening their skills and preparing to lead America into war. As I listened to my father, I couldn't help but wonder if any of those guys had blankets.

Arriving late at night, we checked into our hotel and prepared for the next day, which promised to be a big one. Blankie and I were both excited so it took us awhile to fall asleep but we finally did with visions of The Long Gray Line, as West Pointers are collectively known, marching lockstep in our minds. But when morning came and I stood dressed and ready to go with Blankie in my hands, my father gave me a funny look.

"You can't bring Blankie with us," he said.

"Why not?"

"Well, we're meeting my commanding officer for starters. I don't think General Thayer would look kindly on it."

"What's he got against blankets?" I asked.

"I don't know, but it doesn't matter. It's against Army regulations."

How to Raise a Good Kid

"They have regulations about blankets?"

"They have regulations about everything," he said.

I paused before opining.

"That is really stupid," I said.

Without a choice, I left Blankie behind once again and set out for adventure. The West Point campus was everything my father had promised; big stone buildings and statues with a view of the Hudson River you could stare at for days. General Thayer wasn't all bad either and even took us to lunch in an enormous mess hall, where we ate with all 4000 cadets at the same time. Observing the students together, the General told me that freshmen (plebes as their called) are not allowed to speak unless spoken to by someone older at the table. I told him that things pretty much worked the same way at our house and he seemed to understand. After eating, we toured the sports facilities and even met a few of the coaches. As much as it pained me, I had to admit my father was right. West Point was a pretty spectacular place. I just felt badly that Blankie hadn't seen it with me.

The next day we saw Army play football, another great experience, and then began the long drive home. For much of the ride, I pondered a potential future for myself at West Point. Wouldn't that be something? I thought. Imagine me as part of The Long Gray Line. I might even end up like Patton and Eisenhower and all those other dead guys my father kept talking about. Yes, the life ahead of me was filled with infinite possibilities.

And then we got back. Bounding into the house, I told my mother about all I'd seen before going upstairs to unpack. After witnessing the way cadets keep their dormitories and uniforms, I was ready to commit myself to keeping my own barracks and clothing a bit tidier. But when I opened my suitcase, I made a horrifying discovery: Blankie was nowhere to be found.

Panicked, I raced down to the car and scoured every inch of it to locate my friend. When my search proved fruitless, I ran back inside and breathlessly relayed my plight to my mother.

"It has to be at the hotel," she said, instantly making me feel a bit better.

"You think so?" I asked.

"Yes," she said. "Your father will call right away."

Sure enough, within minutes, my father was on the telephone; first with the front desk and then with housekeeping. He explained the situation and was told they would conduct a thorough search and get back to him.

For hours, I kept a vigil by the telephone. With Blankie missing, I felt paralyzed. In agony, I retraced every one of my steps in my mind and struggled to recall where I might have lost my best friend. How could this have happened on my watch? I bet Eisenhower never lost his blanket. Clearly, I wasn't West Point material.

Finally, the hotel called. No luck. They looked everywhere and even inquired with the chambermaid who cleaned our room. Nobody had seen Blankie. He was gone — ripped from my life forever. Upon receiving the news, I cried harder than I'd ever cried before. My parents tried to comfort me but I was inconsolable. I had let my childhood pal down and there was no way to change it. Somewhere out there was a lonely blanket wondering why I'd cut him loose. I was devastated.

And then I got angry. As I contemplated a future without Blankie, it dawned on me that foul play must have been involved. After all, blankets, even ones as gifted as mine, didn't just up and walk away.

"Dad, did you get rid of Blankie on purpose?" I asked, my lip quivering.

"No," he replied, looking ashen.

"You did, didn't you? You thought I was too old to have a blanket so you threw him out when I wasn't looking."

"That's not true," he said.

"Was it General Thayer?"

"No. General Thayer didn't touch your blanket."

"Then who did?" I asked, demanding an answer.

"I don't know," my father replied.

To this day, I don't know what happened to Blankie at West Point that weekend. Looking back, I see that losing him was one of life's necessary passages. I have a friend who still carries around her childhood doll and it's kind of creepy; so if my father threw Blankie out, I suppose he did me a favor. What happened to me at West Point was just part of growing up, something I knew I had to do even back then when I was a kid. I just wish it hadn't hurt so much.

4
Prejudice

The Power of One

My parents were very involved in our church when I was young. My mother founded a nursery school there and my father was a deacon; so it was common for me to be there three or four times per week. Our family also spent a great deal of time with the minister, Reverend Showalter, his wife and their seven children, several of whom were adopted.

The Showalter's believed in sheltering those who would otherwise go uncared for or abandoned. They infused their congregation with a spirit of community and service to others, and they developed a program to bridge the gap between less fortunate families residing in the city of Rochester, New York and more prosperous ones living in its suburbs.

My parents embraced the program and "adopted" a family living in poverty. The Monroe family consisted of a mother, Viola, and two children, Linda and Jerome. Before long, they were regular visitors to our house and I developed a friendship with Jerome, who was several years older and quickly became a big brother figure to me. The two of us rode bikes, camped out in the backyard and ran around the neighborhood like any two little boys.

As part of the program, our family also made frequent trips to the city, often taking the Monroe children on outings to the zoo and the circus, and visiting them at the holidays to deliver Christmas gifts. I still remember stepping inside their cramped and cluttered apartment for the first time and seeing signs of dilapidation everywhere. I knew immediately it was no place I'd want to live and I felt sorry they had no better option. My parents provided clothes and food and anything else they thought could help make the Monroe's life a bit better.

I was only five years old when this relationship started and the fact that Jerome and his family were black didn't register with me. I had no prejudice I was aware of and saw the Monroe's no differently than my own family except for the absence of a father and money. My parents were teaching me by example to help others without qualification and, frankly, the topic of skin color never came up.

Within two years, we moved away; leaving our church and gradually losing our connection to the Monroe family. The last time I saw Jerome, however, he made an impression on me that would last a lifetime by giving me something he prized but knew I coveted; a black and white yo-yo shaped like a soccer ball that he

How to Raise a Good Kid

carried with him at all times. This act of kindness and generosity meant a great deal to me although I'm sure I didn't sufficiently appreciate at the time how selfless it was given his few material possessions.

Fast forward three years; I am nine and playing pickup football in Randy Olson's backyard with Randy and a small group of kids who reliably show up when called. Randy is a friend from school whose family reminds me a great deal of the Showalter family. Like the Showalter's, the Olson family is large with six kids, several of whom are adopted. And though Mr. Olson is not a minister, he and his wife have strong religious convictions that guide their daily activities and treatment of others; knowledge I've acquired over the course of numerous sleepovers and trips to church with them. Their home is a frequent gathering place for all their children's friends so it is not surprising we assemble there for football.

On the field, we range in age from eight to twelve, and share a common and emerging need to prove ourselves athletically and otherwise as pre-adolescent males. The game is physical and our occasional shouts and grunts are accompanied by jocular taunts. We are trying to impress each other with our words as well as our deeds.

It's January of 1977 and the weather is cold; making everyone's breath visible. The sun is setting and the game is winding down when someone poses an innocent question: "Are you guys going to watch Roots tonight?" — referring to the televised mini-series about the difficult road for blacks from slavery to freedom.

At the time, Roots was an eight-episode television phenomenon drawing over a 100 million viewers a night and, if you said you weren't watching it, you were probably lying. Yet, one of the other boys loudly replied, "Nah, I'm not watching that," with defiance in his voice; like a child refusing to eat vegetables because it was good for him.

I was fascinated by the Roots series, which had been playing for several nights already, and I planned to watch the whole thing. Yet, spurred on by forces I didn't understand, I tried to top the prior boy's remarks by adding, "Yeah, who cares? It's just a bunch of niggers."

My words hung in the frosty air; drawing no reaction from anyone. For a minute, there was dead silence save for the sound of boots crunching snow as we returned to our respective huddles. Any attempt to gauge the reaction of my peers was thwarted by their unwillingness to look my way.

Quickly realizing that my impulsive act of unthinking bravado had failed to impress anyone, I anticipated some form of reprimand and felt relief when it didn't come. This ungainly comfort, however, disappeared seconds later when I looked across the snowy field and saw Randy's sister, Anne, who had been standing on the sidelines watching us play. Anne was one of the Olson's adopted children and she was black. I had forgotten all about her.

Anne's eyes, filled with a combination of disbelief and sadness, told me everything I needed to know about what I'd just done. She looked straight at me and then turned and walked inside the house. As she left, I felt overwhelming embarrassment and shame. I desperately wanted to turn and leave, but I was paralyzed by indecision. Should I knock on the door and apologize or simply wait for Mrs. Olson to come out and punish me; something I was sure would happen once Anne told her what I'd said. Eventually, however, the game ended and I slinked away, having avoided either result. This only made me feel worse knowing that I lacked the bravery to say I was sorry.

Left to ponder why I had used the n-word, I was bereft of a clear answer. It wasn't a word used in my household and I couldn't recall anyone teaching me about it, but somehow I knew the word and knew that speaking it was forbidden; making it strangely attractive. It had the power to shock others which made saying it feel like a dangerous act — the kind that allows a nine-year old boy to explore his world and test its limits. More important, however, I knew the word had the power to hurt others; that black people didn't like to be called by this name, and that it was wrong to say.

I thought of my friend, Jerome, and wondered what, if anything, had changed in the years since I'd seen him last. I felt guilty but, looking within my heart, I saw no ill will or prejudice toward black people whatsoever. I knew I hadn't used the word to demean anyone. To the contrary, insulated by what I believed was a homogenous group of all-white, football friends; I had used it to elicit shock and to prove myself to them by performing a daring deed. I simply hadn't counted on the presence of Randy's sister, Anne.

Still, my experience that day convinced me that the n-word could not be compartmentalized; and that to say it in any setting was to inflict pain on others and shame on yourself. So from that point forward, it never crossed my lips.

5
Self-Expression

The Underwear Dance

My parents had no one to blame but themselves. After all, you don't put a bunk bed in a young boy's room without expecting him to inhabit the top bunk. And it only follows that, within a short period of time, he will choose to do away with the safety bar and sleep only inches from calamity. The rest comes down to temperament. If the boy is the kind who courts danger, he will explore how close to the edge he can get without going over. From there, only one result is possible: a terrifying fall and a potentially serious blow to the head.

My tumble from the top bunk took place with an audience. On an ordinary Friday night, with my parents hosting a dinner party, I was upstairs readying myself for bed when I heard my mother coming up to my room with some guests.

"Come say goodnight to the kids," she said to her friends.

Quickly, and without thinking, I scurried up the wooden step ladder to my elevated lair, spread out on my back, and awaited their impending arrival.

"You're already in bed," my mother said, surprised and pleased to see me up high.

I smiled angelically at her as she stepped into the room with two people who looked vaguely familiar.

"Sweetheart, you remember the Lowell's, right?" she asked.

I nodded.

"You look so cozy up there," Mrs. Lowell said warmly.

"Are those baseball pee jays?" Mr. Lowell asked.

As the adults made small talk and shifted their focus away from me, I sought to regain it.

"Look, Mom," I said, inching toward the unprotected side of the bed.

Unlike others, I wasn't interested in placing myself in peril. I was just showing off.

"Hey, Mom," I called, having failed to turn her head.

"Be careful," she said, glancing my way while continuing her conversation with the Lowell's.

Closer and closer I wriggled until I reached the precipice, with 51% of my body on the mattress and the rest dangling in the air. Still, nobody seemed impressed. Perhaps I need to push things to a new level, I thought. And what better time to do so than now when I've got a full house?

Less than one second later, I passed the point of no return. Plummeting roughly six feet, I hit the floor with a thud; a sound followed immediately by the loudest shriek I'd ever heard. To my surprise, I was unhurt, and I was soon surrounded not only by my mother and the

Lowell's, but everybody in the house as all of my parents' guests made their way upstairs to see about the ruckus. This was an unexpected dividend, and one that I loved.

My appetite for attention was whetted, but falling out of bed was a scary, one-time trick and I needed something less life threatening. So I turned to the time honored tradition of kids everywhere: putting on song and dance shows anytime my parents had company. My sister was a ready participant and served ably as our musical director, wardrobe manager and choreographer. Raiding my parents' record collection, we found an odd assortment of Broadway music and Beatles songs; resulting in an act that was part show tunes, part Strawberry Fields Forever.

We usually opened with (What's the matter with) Kids from the original Bye Bye Birdie cast recording; a snappy number that immediately put the audience (mostly inebriated neighbors) on our side. Next, we moved on to The Beatles 1962-1966 or what everyone called the red album; relying heavily on side one where She Loves You, I Want to Hold Your Hand and All My Loving made for a killer's row of crowd pleasers. Then, in the last part of the performance, we donned hippie outfits and danced dreamily to The Beatles 1967-1970 or what everyone called the blue album; as Lucy in the Sky with Diamonds and Octopus's Garden (during which we intertwined our arms and legs to create the illusion of one creature with eight appendages) brought those assembled to their feet.

All the adulation was quite satisfying for a time, but eventually our routine grew stale in my eyes and I sought more creative freedom. I wanted to do something bigger. I wanted to do something bolder. And, most of all, I wanted to do something on my own, without my sister's accompaniment (think Michael Jackson at Motown 25).

"Don't misunderstand me," I told her. "I don't want to tear our act apart. I just want to stretch it out."

To her credit, my sister understood my desire to stretch, but when she asked me how I planned to do it, I didn't have a good answer. Fortunately, fate would intervene days later when I saw an advertisement on television offering twenty hit songs by twenty original artists on a single record. It seemed a little too good to be true, but after hearing a snippet of Tie a Yellow Ribbon Round the Ole Oak Tree I was sold and started begging my mother to call the telephone number I'd written down and order the collection.

I still remember how excited I was the day it arrived. At the age of seven, receiving anything in the mail was a miraculous experience and it went double this time as I marveled at the package's sudden appearance.

Placing my new set of super hits on our portable turntable, I began searching for a song that could catapult me from living room star to Vegas headliner. My hunt began slowly as I listened to Rikki Don't Lose That Number and Midnight at the Oasis, and wondered how two such awful songs ever became popular. They were slow and plodding and impossible to dance to in my estimation. In contrast, Billy Don't Be a Hero had some very good moments, but I wanted something truly great, and a little further into the record I found it.

The second I heard Billy Preston's Nothing from Nothing, I fell in love. It started with a riff of playful, organ-generated horns before jumping headfirst into an irresistible piano groove. The music was joyous, raucous and unlike anything my ears had ever experienced. It made me happy instantly and I knew it deserved its own special dance for our production.

Thanks to the song's unconventional lyrics, however, it took me awhile to figure out what that dance would be. On its face, it was a song about subtraction. "Nothin' from nothin' leaves nothin'," Preston sang. But clearly math was not foremost on the his mind. Amidst the frenetic rhythm and the infectious beat, there was a message about romantic relationships, a topic I knew nothing about. "You gotta have somethin' if you wanna be with me," he insisted.

Unable to decipher its true meaning, I decided I would honor the spirit of the song; and hence was born The Underwear Dance. The Underwear Dance had three critical elements: chaos, nudity and madness; and it soon became our signature show closer.

After the Broadway and Beatles portions of our repertoire were done, my sister would keep the living room crowd (the same inebriated neighbors I mentioned before) warm with charming banter while I retreated upstairs for a costume change.

My transformation was always quick as it only required me to strip down to my underwear and then stuff my tighty whities with every other pair of underwear I owned (roughly 15-20 pairs) until I was bulging with lumps. As soon as I was done, I called down to my sister from the second floor. "Ready!" And she would start the music.

With the boogie fever of Billy Preston's piano spreading like the flu at a day care center, I soared down the stairs and took the makeshift stage; my arms and legs flailing in all directions. If the sight of a small, semi-clad boy didn't take their breath away, what happened next always did. Dancing wildly, like James Brown himself had gotten hold of me, I reached into my underwear and, one by one, began flinging the other pairs of underwear into the audience. "Nothin' from nothin' leaves nothin'," I sang, as a snowstorm of briefs came down from the sky. "You gotta have somethin', if you wanna be with me. I'm not tryin' to be your hero. 'Cause that zero is too low for me." Uncertain of what was happening, many in the crowd took cover as anarchy reigned.

Eventually, everyone caught on to the fun and began flinging the rogue underwear at each other. Once I shed all my Fruit-of-the-Looms, I took my bows to rapturous applause; returning to my bedroom drained but satisfied. The addition of The Underwear Dance to our show was an unquestionable success and I performed it many times to great effect. Yet, over the coming months, as I began to feel the pressure to top it, I realized there was no place to go as an artist. As things stood, only one thin piece of cotton separated me from an all-nude act and I had no intention of going in that direction. Faced with no viable alternative, I did what every performer dreams of doing: I retired at the top; a few weeks shy of my eighth birthday.

When I look back, what I learned from the experience was one simple but invaluable lesson: if you're going to dance in your underwear, make sure to keep it on and keep it clean.

6
How to Handle a Bully

The WHO Club

In fifth grade, I fell prey to a hate group. It wasn't the KKK or the Aryan Nation or even the Junior League. It was the WHO Club whose acronym stood simply for We Hate O'Dwyer. Like many entities dedicated to hate, the WHO Club was a splinter organization having originally started as WHOPID; an assemblage committed to destroying my life and those of Kenny Pietrowski, Tommy Indovino and Steve Danesi. Soon thereafter, for reasons that have never been disclosed, WHOPID released the others from its fatwa and focused solely on me.

The leader of the WHO Club was Dirk Brody, a short, fat tyrant with a hair-trigger temper; though to be fair we were all short back then. Like most sociopaths, Dirk could be charming, generous to a fault and fun at kiddie birthday parties, which were the qualities that originally attracted me to him. We started out as friends; hanging out and having sleepovers, and we grew quite close until one fateful day.

Down in Dirk's basement and deep into a three-week game of Risk, I amassed my armies at the border of Kamchatka, a region Dirk controlled. Woefully outmanned, he realized I was close to achieving the game's objective — total world domination. Rather than let that occur, Dirk threw a fit and flipped the board in the air; sending pieces flying everywhere. "I don't want to play anymore," he huffed, nearly at the point of tears. Game over.

This episode might have been the end of it, but what happened next took our fractured friendship and snapped it clean in half. At school the next week, Dirk became aware that I was going out with Kathy Collins, the prettiest girl in our class. Going out with someone back then didn't have much practical application in day to day life; it was basically a public acknowledgement by two people that they liked each other better than anyone else and, presumably if the world was to suddenly implode, they would prefer to be buried together holding hands. Dirk, however, didn't see it as something insignificant. I now had something that he wanted and he was going to take it from me by any means necessary.

He approached me with a simple proposition. Break things off with Kathy Collins and he would give me an entire pack of sour apple Now-n-Laters or other candy of my choice. When sugar-coated bribery didn't work, Dirk immediately moved on to something out of Godfather 2 and told me that if I didn't end my relationship with

How to Raise a Good Kid

Kathy, he would start a hate club targeting me and my friends. Once again, I refused.

Machiavellian to the core, Dirk made good on his word; birthing WHOPID and beginning a campaign of disinformation about me and my associates. After abbreviating to WHO and concentrating his efforts on me alone, he began scrawling the acronym in black magic marker on any open space he could find in and out of the classroom; from the back of chairs to book covers; from desktops to blackboards. Before long, I saw it everywhere I looked, but ignored it; confident Dirk would lose enthusiasm for the endeavor and the situation would dissipate. Unfortunately, this was a gross miscalculation on my part.

Soon, Dirk recruited others to his cause by telling them things about me that weren't true; convincing them I'd said things behind their back in a ruse too sophisticated for me to figure out at the age of ten. All I knew was that more and more kids seemed to be avoiding me and the WHO scribblings in black ink were multiplying.

Worse yet, like any evil ruler, Dirk had henchman; namely Timmy "Meat Cleaver" Maroney, a butcher's son, and Ed "Baldy" Baldritch, a cop's kid, who did Dirk's bidding. Every time Ms. Cox, our teacher, took us from our homeroom to the cafeteria, music class or elsewhere, Meat Cleaver and Baldy found me in line as we moved through the school's corridors and shoved, punched and verbally taunted me as much as they could before we arrived at our destination. Previously innocent phrases like, "It's time for art class everyone," now sent a chill down my spine. Every day was full of panic and dread.

Still, I was determined to solve this problem on my

own. For weeks, as my plight worsened, I remained glumly silent as did everyone else in my class. Ms. Cox was oblivious to it all despite the WHO markings, now ubiquitous, and the obvious change in my persona from extrovert to basket case. I feared it would never end but, perversely, the longer it went on, the more something in me wanted to endure it just to show Dirk he couldn't break me. So I said nothing in school and I said nothing at home until one Friday night as I got ready for bed after a long week of constant harassment.

Sensing something was terribly wrong with her little boy; my mother sat on the edge of my bed and gently asked me to open up to her. When I tried to explain, my emotions overwhelmed me. Tears quickly evolved into heavy sobs and prevented me from getting the words out. For two months, I had kept everything to myself, but now the pain of the experience; of being ostracized from my classmates; of being hated for reasons I didn't understand, consumed me. When I finally explained the circumstances, my mother was appalled and vowed to rectify things. Still clinging to my innate sense of self-reliance, I begged her not to do anything and she promised she wouldn't. But I would be a liar if I said I wasn't pleased with what happened the following Monday morning.

Settling into my desk five minutes before school was scheduled to start; I was amazed to see my father suddenly stride into my class. He was wearing a suit and his favorite top coat, and he glanced at me briefly before conferring with Ms. Cox. He then walked over to Dirk, took him by the hand and physically removed him from the room. For the first time ever, I actually felt sorry for my tormentor as I knew what was coming next. My father, a big man with a prosecutor's demeanor, was not someone you wanted to anger. His scoldings, more accurately described as withering face-melters, were legendary. In short, I knew Dirk was in some serious dog doo.

I never found out what was said in the coat room, but Dirk Brody never bothered me again. Returning to class, his face flush and his eyes watering, Dirk slumped into his seat like a defeated foe. That afternoon, with the assistance of Meat Cleaver and Baldy, he cleaned up all the graffiti and the WHO Club was no more. The story, though, wasn't over.

During the next seven years, as we passed into junior high and then high school, Dirk and I traveled in separate circles and had relatively little contact. Senior year, however, Dirk had his heart set on attending a particular college. Having submitted his application, he was informed by his dream school that he would need to interview with a randomly assigned local alum as part of the process. Soon thereafter, Dirk entered the alum's downtown office and uttered the words still famous in our household: "Mr. O'Dwyer, I'm Dirk Brody. You may remember me."

I assure you my father did.

7
Popularity

Spellcheck

It was an ordinary day in sixth grade when my teacher, Mrs. Shears, walked our class to gym. June had arrived and I was feeling particularly good because school superlatives were announced that morning and I'd been named best speller; an award for which I received a book of crossword puzzles. I really wanted to win most popular but I took pride in my spelling prowess and felt confident that a life of words would be a good one.

In the school locker room, I found myself dressing next to Gary Clark, a free spirit with an easy grin and a natural talent for defying authority. Gary had been officially designated class clown earlier in the day as well as most likely to burn the school down in an informal poll. He was the son of the school board president and part of a devoutly Catholic family; so naturally he'd never met a rule he didn't want to demolish.

Unaccustomed to rebellion of any kind, I was wary of Gary; yet something about his willingness to challenge the pre-determined order of things appealed to me. He was constantly sticking his hand into the proverbial fire and didn't seem to care if he got burned so long as he had fun in the process. Other than my Uncle Henry, who spent most of our family Thanksgivings passed out on the couch, I'd never met anyone who looked at the world this way.

Inside the gymnasium, Mr. Davidson, an older teacher with a hangdog expression permanently affixed to his face, divided the boys from the girls and put us on opposite walls facing each other. Standing in the middle, equidistant to both groups, he announced that we'd be square dancing; a proclamation met with a groan. He then proceeded toward a storage room where he kept the stereo equipment and speakers leaving us alone for a few dangerous minutes.

As soon as Mr. Davidson began walking away, Gary tapped me on the shoulder and said something that changed me forever.

"Theresa and Lexie want us to moon them," he said.

Theresa Nelson and Lexie Papadopolous were two girls who'd developed early and thus drew more than their fair share of attention from the boys.

"They do?" I asked, proud that I knew what it meant to moon someone.

"Definitely," Gary said. "They told me before class."
"Are you sure?"
"Yes. Just look at them."

How to Raise a Good Kid 43

Gazing in their direction, I could see Theresa and Lexie looking back at us; whispering and giggling all the while.

"Quick; before Davidson gets back," Gary demanded. "On the count of three. One. . . . Two. . . ."

"Wait a minute, Gary. I'm not ready yet," I stammered, nervously looking around to see if our teacher was returning.

"You want Theresa and Lexie to think you're cool, right?" Gary asked.

"Of course," I said.

"And wouldn't you like to be the most popular kid in school?" he asked.

"Well, yes, but I'm already the best speller. I don't want to be greedy."

"I guarantee this will make you the most popular kid in the whole school," Gary said. "Maybe the world."

"The whole world?" I asked.

"Yup."

The gym was hot and I felt faint.

"I'm not sure this is a good idea," I said.

"Let's go," Gary urged. "Let's do this!"

Sweaty, conflicted and standing on the precipice of pure anarchy, I willfully stepped over the ledge. In complete defiance of what I knew was right, I spun around in tandem with Gary and dropped my pants in Theresa and Lexie's general direction. It was over in a literal flash but there was no doubt we'd served up two full moons with all the fixins as Gary later described it.

When it was over, I was exhilarated; a full-blooded criminal. I'd done something bad and I liked it. Even better, I'd gotten away with it. By the time Mr. Davidson returned with the stereo equipment, we were doing nothing but basking in the newfound glory bestowed upon us by Theresa, Lexie and the rest of our classmates who thought our stunt was hysterical. There were waves, smiles and countless other acts of good will raining down on us. We weren't mere mortals anymore. We were legends. The rest of gym class was an adrenaline-juiced joy ride. I was promenading and do-si-do-ing like I'd never done before; cocksure like a cowboy. Why I hadn't walked on the wild side before escaped me.

Back in the locker room, Gary and I were surrounded like two pied pipers as we regaled our fellow classmates with the tale of our perfect crime. It was shortly into the story when I realized that Mr. Davidson had joined our circle and, by the look on his face, I knew he wasn't there to collect towels.

"Mr. Clark and Mr. O'Dwyer, may I see you?" he asked, signaling us to follow him toward his office.

Oh, no, what have I done? I thought, as I walked behind him, my head bowed and my body quaking.

"Theresa and Lexie told me that you mooned them. Is that true?" Mr. Davidson asked.

After a moment's silence, Gary and I spoke up at the same time. He said, "No," and I said, "Yes." Clearly, my inexperience as a criminal wasn't doing us any favors.

"Well, which is it? Yes or no?" Mr. Davidson asked. "Tell you what. I think I'm going to let Mr. Stoller sort this out."

The next thing I knew I was sitting in the waiting area outside Principal Stoller's office, every molecule in me brimming with dread. How could I be so reckless? I wondered. Why did Theresa and Lexie tell on us? Didn't they know I was the school's best speller?

How to Raise a Good Kid

Gary, for his part, was completely undaunted. He'd been through this routine before and knew he'd survive both Stoller's and his father's wrath. As for me, I wasn't so sure. After Principal Stoller expressed how disappointed he was in my behavior, he said he'd reached my mother at work and that she was coming to pick me up. This made the interminable minutes until her arrival measurably more tolerable because I knew she'd defer punishment for my actions to my father and, sure enough, she said little to me as we got in the car.

Back at home, my mother sent me up to my room and told me to wait for my father to return from work. It was then the full implications of what I'd done began to register. I spent the next two hours imagining the price I would pay for being an outlaw. There would be spanking. There would be grounding. There would be a suspension of all privileges. There would be chores and perhaps a stint at Attica.

From my window, I finally saw my father driving up and felt my veins fill with freshly pumped fear. A minute later, I heard the door to the garage slam shut and the sound of my father's wingtips hitting the hardwood floor in our kitchen. My heart pounded as I strained to hear my parents chatting downstairs about the events of the day. Any second now, she would tell him and I would be beckoned. The anticipation was excruciating. A part of me just wanted it to be over, whatever the consequences.

And then a funny thing happened: a half hour went by without a word from anyone. This was highly unusual; unprecedented in fact. My father never let matters of discipline linger, particularly ones of this magnitude. What was going on? After a full hour passed, it dawned on me. This was part of the punishment. They knew that leaving me alone with my thoughts would be the perfect prelude to the real punishment; an appetizer of sorts. It was diabolically simple but brilliant.

Eventually, however, my mother called me for dinner and I cautiously made my way out of my room to join them at the table. Now I'm in for it, I thought. But food was served and drinks were poured and still nothing was said about what I'd done. It was maddening. I kept waiting for one of them to raise the issue but they didn't; letting the sword of Damocles hang over my head a bit longer.

After dinner, I did my homework; wondering every minute when my punishment would arrive. Didn't they know how much I was suffering? At bedtime, they each came in and kissed me good night before closing my door and leaving me alone in the darkness. I couldn't believe it. They hadn't said a word. I'd actually gotten away with the whole thing. Maybe with a few more stunts, I could solidify my status as most popular, I thought. Suddenly, however, my door opened and I froze beneath my sheets. My father stood in the doorway, his large silhouette framed by the hall light.

"Do me a favor, okay?" he asked, tersely.

"Sure, Dad," I replied; panic in my throat.

"Don't pull your pants down at school, all right?"

"Got it, Dad. I promise," I said, thereby ending my life of crime and my pursuit of popularity forever.

8
Courage

Love, Joy and Sheer Terror

It was a match made far from heaven — my mother, the world's most cautious woman, and ski racing. Yet there she stood at the starter's gate in her canary yellow ski togs like Franz Klammer at the 1976 Olympics in Innsbruck. Today, many years later, I marvel that it ever really happened. But it did — five times in fact — right before my eyes. Only now do I understand its impact on me.

My mother hates to be cold — always has. When you go to the beach and see a woman under a blanket warding off the chill, that's her. She also hates going fast. If you've been stuck behind the driver who refuses to go more than 55 mph no matter how much you tailgate or honk your horn, you're familiar with her work and will understand why her former stint as a competitive downhiller is so confounding at first glance.

The blame lay with my father, an avid skier who relocated (some say kidnapped) her to Rochester, a city at the center of western New York's snow-belt between Syracuse and Buffalo. After teaching my mother the sport at various scattered venues, he set about finding a convenient and inexpensive place where they could regularly enjoy his favorite pastime. The birth of two children temporarily slowed his progress, but as soon as my sister and I were old enough to tackle a bunny slope, the search resumed.

Hunt Hollow, a ski club located in Naples, New York, was set amid the beautiful Bristol Hills in the Finger Lakes Region. Less than an hour south of Rochester, Naples was semi-famous as the birthplace of New York's wine industry and the home of the annual Grape Festival. It also offered the some of the state's best skiing west of Lake Placid.

My father signed up for a family membership that allowed us to ski as much as we wanted and, at first, enthusiasm was robust. The scenery was beautiful, the skiing was fun and my mother could escape to a chair by the fireplace in the club's lodge whenever her hands and feet began to turn blue. There was also an abundance of families just like ours who contributed to the palpable camaraderie in the lift lines and inside the lodge, a spacious, pinewood expanse, where people cooked up large vats of chili to share and cracked open oversized thermoses containing coffee and hot chocolate.

Soon we were going every Saturday and Sunday throughout the winter from 7:00 a.m. until dusk. Although I was too young to appreciate it then, Hunt

How to Raise a Good Kid

Hollow was a protective bubble of sorts — a place that provided parents with two days of respite from the ever-worsening economic news of the late 1970's and a chance to move freely; unchained to kids who were anxious to ski with their friends but willing to circle back at lunch time. I remember walking into the lodge around noon on many occasions to find a makeshift Dixieland jazz band playing with my father out in front singing; a beer in one hand and a microphone in the other. His bulky yellow parka and voice were unmistakable as I came through the door, walking awkwardly in ski boots, and I could only stop and watch in amazement as he showed me what enjoying life was all about.

Unfortunately, the peak experience of Hunt Hollow couldn't last — and it didn't. By the third winter, the novelty was gone and my family's solidarity on ski weekends began to splinter. My father still wanted to go every Saturday and Sunday, but my sister and I, thirteen and eleven respectively by then, had other ideas. Getting up at dawn had lost its allure and our gratitude for how lucky we were to be skiing and not working in a coal mine began to be lost on us in our adolescent state. Invitations from friends to do other things began to compete with and intrude on our regular trips to Naples, creating friction with my father who wanted the world to remain as it had been.

My father's intentions were good. He knew that skiing got us out of the house and away from the television, and forced us to break a sweat. Hunt Hollow, however, meant a lot more to him than that. For my father, these ski weekends represented a final frontier in his efforts to keep his family together as a cohesive unit. On the cusp of having two teenagers, he felt the tenuous grasp of parental control being wrested away by outside forces and he wasn't going down without a fight.

My mother remained silent, but she was thrilled by the prospect of a bit less skiing. As we ate breakfast by the television and listened to the weather report at 6:00 a.m. on a typical Saturday morning, her body language alone told me she was rooting for road closures due to inclement conditions. Still, whenever conflict over our weekend plans arose, she stayed neutral; mediating between the parties to reach a compromise that would satisfy both her husband and her children. And this approach worked for awhile until the number of times my sister and I begged off began to frustrate my father.

In addition to all the implications for family togetherness, this was also an issue of economics. My father had paid a few thousand dollars for his family's ability to ski on an unlimited basis and, like Popeye at an all-you-can-eat spinach bar; he was going to get his money's worth.

"I've signed us all up for the Lovejoy Series," he announced excitedly as we drove home one weekend after skiing together for the first time in a few weeks.

"The what?" my mother asked.

"The Lovejoy Race Series. You've heard me mention it before," my father said, pretending to be surprised it hadn't crossed my mother's radar before while she was stirring vats of chili in the lodge.

The Lovejoy Race Series was a ski racing competition between members; spread over seven consecutive weekends at the club. Named for Frank Lovejoy, a doctor and the visionary behind Hunt Hollow, the series required skiers to participate in no less than five of the seven races in order to qualify to win. By entering the whole family, my father, in a plot the CIA could admire, guaranteed himself at least five more family weekends that winter.

"Dad, are you serious?" I asked. "I don't want to race."

"Dad, get real," my sister said, trotting out her favorite catch-phrase.

"You guys are going to love it," my father insisted.

"You signed up all of us?" my mother asked, still hopeful she'd been spared.

"Yep. We're all racing."

To put things in perspective, this was akin to being enrolled in the Marine Corps without your consent. And the equivalent of boot camp at Parris Island began the next week with the arrival of the first race. Naturally, blizzard-like weather was expected.

My mother, who'd never been in a competitive bake-off let alone a ski race, was terrified. My father told her that ski racing would require her to abandon all of her inhibitions and fears, items she'd been clinging to tightly for nearly forty years.

"To really be good, you must have a complete disregard for your own personal safety and be willing to live on the edge of calamity at all times," my father explained, having watched ABC's Wide World of Sports a few too many times.

"What if your goal is just to make it down alive?" my mother asked.

To ease her anxiety as well as my own, I assisted my mother with pre-race preparations by making sure her bindings, boots and poles were in perfect working order, and getting her skis waxed. We then skied together alongside the empty race course early in the morning;

stopping every fifty feet so I could show her the trickier gates in the course's layout. I was familiar with the format of the giant slalom from television and knew the turns were more forgiving than in pure slalom; a small blessing for both of us. We even adopted a theme song for our troubles: Paul Simon's Slip Sliding Away.

When the time arrived to race, we shuffled through the lift line, each step taking us closer to our mutually dreaded destination: the starter's hut at the top of the mountain. Of course, by now, my sister was nowhere to be found, having brilliantly negotiated her way out of the situation by telling my father she was experiencing female troubles. Atrocious weather, however, was very much with us as we took our seats in a dual chairlift and pulled the safety bar down in front of us. Gale force winds whipped the snow around like a blender shredding coconut and reduced visibility to zero. I was genuinely miserable but my mother, who had a look of terror on her face and was shivering so much her teeth were chattering, was catatonic.

"It's going to be okay, Mom," I said, managing to mask my own sense of doom for a minute. "We only have to do this four more times after today," I added, no doubt making her feel even worse.

At the summit, where my father awaited us, adults lined up to take their turn before the kids. The men went first, each passing through a small wooden hut located on a rise until they stood at the starter's gate where a wand, once tripped, would trigger a stop clock and time each run. The women were next and as my mother joined the queue, I saw she was one of only two in the whole club who'd decided to participate. Watching her

How to Raise a Good Kid

take off down the steep ramp from the starter's gate and toward the first set of flags, I felt an undeniable pride. As she disappeared into an endless white void, I prayed that somehow, someway, she would make it down the hill and finish the race. And, to my great satisfaction, she did. I did, too, and immediately upon finding each other in the lodge afterwards and exchanging survival stories, we began worrying about the next one.

Before long, after our second, third and fourth suicide missions were successfully completed in the weeks that followed; we finally saw the last hurdle in Frank Lovejoy's sadistic, snowy track meet: the fifth and final race. For my mother, the stakes were high. As my father had reminded her repeatedly, she would win the second place trophy if she could simply finish since there were only two women competing. Of course, given the notoriously icy nature of New York skiing, finishing was never a sure thing. Each race was treacherous, and with a single slip of a ski, it was easy to post a DNF (Did Not Finish) or a DSQ (Disqualified).

On the day of fateful number five, my mother rode the chairlift with me. She looked more nervous than usual, but when her turn to ski arrived, she passed uneventfully through the starter's hut and took her place at the starter's gate, pausing briefly to adjust her goggles. As the final adult competitor, her every move was under the close scrutiny of the forty or so kids, including me, who stood together waiting for their turn to race.

And then it happened. Launching herself through the starter's gate, my mother skied off the ramp in the wrong direction and smashed directly into a large tree; toppling over and landing down in the well created by the frozen drifts surrounding its trunk. Stunned for an instant, I quickly got out of my bindings and began to climb down toward where she lay to try and help her up. As I did, I heard a sound I will never forget.

All the kids who had just witnessed my mother's mishap were laughing at her. And as I walked toward her, the sound continued to grow; louder and louder. They found her misfortune entertaining and perhaps I would have, too, if it hadn't been my mother at the bottom of that tree. But there was nothing about this that I found funny and, unexpectedly, my eyes welled up with tears. I felt so sorry for my mother and it wasn't just because she had fallen. It was because I knew the back story. I knew how much she didn't want to be there in the first place. I knew she had only agreed to enter these races to make my father happy and to keep the family peace. I knew she didn't care one wit about the Lovejoy Race Series or a second place trophy. She only cared about us. In the face of having to do something she didn't want to do, she never complained. She never quit. And, despite her fears, she was one race away from beating them. In doing all this, she had taught me all I'd ever need to know about courage.

With the clock still running, my mother climbed out of that tree well, stutter-stepped twenty feet back up the mountain and skied off in the direction of the first gate. She finished the race and took second place that year in women's division of the Lovejoy Race Series. If you go to Hunt Hollow today, you can still find her name on the wall.

9
First Crushes

The Act of Hot Pursuit

Finding a girlfriend is difficult when you're a kid. Picture a six-year old boy riding shotgun in a station wagon; his head hanging out the passenger window like a puppy's as his mother navigates the tight turns of an apartment complex parking lot. He is determined to deliver a birthday gift to Mrs. Austin, his first grade teacher and one true love, and nothing will stop him. In 1973, that boy was me.

With no fear, I got out of the car and walked toward Mrs. Austin's door. In one hand, I held a rose. In the other — a poorly wrapped bottle of Charlie cologne spray. I'm not sure what I expected to happen. I had no plan for what I would do after I presented the gifts. It never occurred to me that Mrs. Austin's existing marriage or our 28-year age gap would prevent us from starting a relationship. Of course, it was over quickly. She acted suitably surprised and grateful and then politely excused herself; closing the door and leaving me on the front stoop wondering what had just happened. Devoid of an invitation to come inside, I schlepped back to my mother's car having just learned the first rule of love: some relationships are doomed from the start.

Fortunately, second grade arrived like a new poker hand and I stood ready to put my chips down again. This time, I set my sights on someone more age appropriate — Julie Cardell — who was in my class and unmarried from what I could tell. Still new to the game, I had no qualms about immediately professing my undying love for her; an approach that rarely works I would later discover. Julie, however, seemed flattered and always met my words of affection with an enthusiastic smile. Things looked promising and I began to make plans for our future together. I even looked up Julie's address in the phone book and had my mom drive me by her house — a technique I hadn't given up on despite the prior debacle at Mrs. Austin's place. This time, I stayed in the car and asked my mom to loop around the circle that led to the Cardell's driveway. To me, it was reconnaissance. Today, I suppose they'd call it stalking. Either way, I was convinced Julie and I would be together forever.

In retrospect, I never saw my competition coming; namely Steve Parker, a fellow classmate. Suddenly, I wasn't the only one vying for Julie's attention and my insecurity began to show. Every day, I asked Julie who she liked better — Steve or me. And every day, she told me that she really liked both of us but, if forced to choose, she would have to pick Steve. Continuing for months, her rejection gave me a complex. How could she like him more than me? It made no sense. Sure, Steve had hair the color of corn silk and looked like the offspring of an Icelandic Viking and a Swedish supermodel, but the Julie I knew wasn't impressed by physical appearance or other shallow considerations. After all, I'd driven by her house and was certain that its modest, understated exterior was an accurate gauge of the values being taught inside its four walls. Apparently, I was wrong and by the age of seven, I understood all too well the pain of being in love with someone who isn't in love with you. Overnight, all the songs on the radio by Bread and Roberta Flack made sense to me. My only relief: Julie Cardell moved away the summer after second grade.

Entering third grade and feeling disillusioned about love, I exiled myself to the romantic hinterlands. Having struck out twice, I decided to ignore girls and focus primarily on my studies; a good decision considering the challenging curriculum ahead of cursive writing, times tables and snack time. Love would have to wait until I learned enough marketable skills to attract and retain a wife. Of course, the best laid plans rarely proceed without a hitch and mine were no exception as I soon developed a crush on my teacher, Ms. Richardson, who was sweet, sophisticated and, curse my luck, engaged to be married. Prepared to fight for her 'til the death, I gave up immediately once she announced she was joining the Peace Corps and moving to Uganda. Even I knew we didn't stand a chance with a continent between us; a point made all too poignantly when she showed me how to paper-mache a topographical map of Africa during our geography unit.

Heartbroken and questioning my will to carry on, I reluctantly showed up for fourth grade. By now, a career in the priesthood sounded appealing and, when asked to draw a self-portrait for parents' night, I depicted myself in a brown robe and sandals. Uncertain if I was well-suited to a monastic existence as a non-Catholic, I started sitting alone at lunch and giving my dessert away to see how good I was at sacrifice; a practice I kept up for a solid four days. Lonely and a few pounds lighter, I experienced a miracle when a new girl arrived at school and I instantly fell in love with her. All I knew about Casey Cross was that she was beautiful and had moved to Rochester from a foreign country called California. Renouncing my plans for the priesthood, I made it my sole purpose in life to make her mine.

Getting close to Casey proved a challenge. We were in two separate classes that rarely interacted so I was limited at first to gazing at her from across the lunchroom and wondering whether she liked bologna and cheese with the crusts cut off as much as I did. Not long after her arrival, the gods smiled down on me when it was announced there would be something called an Activity Night for the whole fourth grade. I had never heard of an Activity Night but if it gave me a chance to spend time in proximity to Casey without having to do any math, I was all for it.

As it turned out, Activity Night was nothing more than an evening spent at school taking part in various gym activities such as dodgeball, square dancing and roller-skating. Upon arrival, I took my place on the far side of the gym with all the other boys and began scouting the line-up of girls assembled 200-feet across from us. There, in a green sweater and black-n-white checked skirt, was Casey. My heart thumped as Mrs. Livingston, the gym teacher, divided us into groups for square dancing. Please let me be in her group, I silently pleaded. Of course, no such fortune befell me. So while Casey dosy-doed Richie Resnick and swung Jack Bartholomew, I watched helplessly from my adjacent square and began plotting Plan B.

The last activity of the night was roller-skating in a large circle around the gym — a perfect opportunity for me to engage my target. I knew the school would do nothing to assist me such as dim the lights or play slow, romantic music but, undeterred, I strapped on my skates and set out to find Casey; entering the traffic circle as it swirled in front of me. Soon, I saw her and her friends making their way around the loop; occasionally using each other as support and laughing the entire time. Slowly but surely I closed the gap until she was no more than ten feet ahead of me. Round and round we went; the bright lights and blaring sounds of ABBA adding to the drama.

Suddenly, I had my opening. One of Casey's friends peeled off toward the water fountain, leaving Casey's right flank open. Just a few more feet to go, I thought; willing my skates to move more quickly. To pull even with the girl of my dreams, I needed one single burst of energy. A poor skater, I had no business trying to go faster, but it was now or never and I chose now.

Focusing all my concentration on my skates, I pushed off harder than usual. First with my left skate — then my right — left — right — left –right. But with adrenaline shooting through me like rapids through a riverbed, I pushed too hard. And instead of generating enough speed to pull even with Casey, I knew right away I was going to shoot past her. Attempting to salvage the operation, I called out to her breathlessly as I whizzed by: "Casey, would you like to skate with meeeeeeeee?" Unfortunately, the opportunity was blown. Losing control of my speed and my skates simultaneously, I flew out of the circle and crashed into the gym's cinderblock wall. My helmet-less head took the brunt of the collision; leaving me dizzy and disoriented on the hardwood floor. Next thing I knew, I was being carried to the nurse's office by a group of teachers and chaperones. My humiliation was eclipsed only by my feeling of failure.

Activity Night was on a Friday so I had a whole weekend to mull what went wrong and contemplate what I could have done differently. Anticipating judgmental stares and cruel jokes at my expense, I didn't want to go to school on Monday. But when I climbed on the bus that morning with the encouragement of my parents, something wonderful began to happen.

"Hey, O'Dwyer," Eric Olson, a fellow fourth-grader, said. "I hear you're going out with Casey Cross."

"What?" I asked.

"Going out" was the phrase used to indicate two people liked each other and had agreed to be boyfriend and girlfriend.

"I heard that you asked her to go out with you at the Activity Night and she said yes," Eric continued.

"She did?"

"That's what I heard," he said. "Nice job."

"Thanks," I said, completely bewildered.

Now going out with someone was a very big deal.

So big, I found myself on the horns of a moral dilemma. I knew what Eric Olson was saying wasn't true, but I didn't see the harm in letting this fantastic rumor percolate awhile longer.

Once at school, I experienced the same thing repeatedly as one person after another congratulated me for successfully convincing Casey to go out with me. Could it possibly be true? Could she have interpreted my request to skate with her as an invitation to be my girlfriend? This wasn't so far-fetched. Having misheard my question, perhaps she said yes, but was drowned out by the sound of my head hitting cinderblock. These were all distinct possibilities. And as the day went on and neither Casey nor any of her representatives corrected the record, I chose to believe that we were indeed going out.

I felt elated. After many years of searching, I had my first girlfriend at last. Unfortunately, within a very short period of time, my elation evaporated as the uncertainty surrounding our coupling began to haunt me. In my heart, I didn't know whether Casey was my girlfriend or not and I felt both powerless and afraid to find out the truth. Back then, the strange thing about going out with someone in the fourth grade was that you never talked to them; especially if they weren't in your class. And since Casey had a different teacher than me, and Twitter, text pages and cell phones didn't exist, my communication with her was limited to sneaking glances when we'd pass in the hallway.

Admittedly, I could've called Casey from home at night, but that would've required me to speak to her parents; a mountain I was nowhere near ready to climb. Besides, a big part of me didn't want to give her the opportunity to break things off. And so I began avoiding her; a move that only made me feel worse as the weeks went on. Several months later, a friend told me that he had heard from a friend of another friend that Casey had broken up with me. It hurt, but I tried to be philosophical about it. When it comes to love, I'd heard you never know what you've got 'til it's gone. But in this case, I still didn't know.

A year later, in fifth grade, I met Kathy Collins who became my first official girlfriend; one that I talked to, took to the movies and eventually kissed — on a hill behind the school under an armada of stars after sneaking out of another Activity Night. This time it felt just right. Love had triumphed once again.

10
Hard Work

Up Against the Snow Fence

My father's darkest fear, the one that kept him up at night, was the prospect of raising spoiled, lazy children. He worried that too many tennis lessons, ski trips and pool clubs would give us a sense of entitlement that would be crippling when we got out in the unforgiving world, and he was determined not to let that happen. As he explained it once, he wanted to give us a happy childhood; just not too happy.

To avoid burdening society with two more bums, my father did a number of ingenious things to my sister and me. The first was to tell us over and over that we better fly when pushed out of the nest. He would pay for our schooling but after that we were on our own. In his words, he didn't want us coming back to him for "one red cent" after graduation. I heard this speech for the first time at age five and every week from that point forward so by high school it was deeply embedded in my brain.

My father also repeated ad nauseam that we would never inherit a single dollar from him. He planned to spend whatever he and my mother had so we should never let our minds ponder, for even an instant, the possibility of coming into money. Along with this warning came his guarantee that he would never buy us a car, give us a credit card or provide an allowance. Money would be handed out on an as-needed basis and only for legitimate expenses like band uniforms or appendectomies.

Continually schooling us in these hard realities, my father simultaneously assigned long lists of chores that had to be completed prior to the commencement of self-indulgent activities like watching television or eating breakfast. He had his own way of torturing my sister, but for me he turned the boundaries of our yard into a Soviet-era labor camp every weekend.

Saturday mornings started at 6:00 a.m. with the sounds of the West Point marching band echoing throughout our house. Seconds later, my bedroom door would open and my father would inform me it was time to get up just in case the military music hadn't tipped me off. Resistance was pointless so I dutifully got dressed and readied myself for whatever unpleasant activities awaited me outside.

From the time I was seven, we lived in the country without another house in sight; and our property, most of it covered in weeds, wild flowers and foot-long grass, went on forever. The size and scope of the land meant every season held daunting tasks, but none was worse than winter when wind chills regularly sent the

How to Raise a Good Kid

temperature well below zero. This was Western New York in the late 1970's. The landscape was bleak and if you squinted hard enough, you could see Siberia.

The winter job I dreaded the most, by far, was putting up our snow fence every year. For those who don't know, a snow fence is a barrier temporarily erected to catch snow and prevent it from piling up so heavily on an adjacent road that cars can't pass. In our case, the road being protected along which the fence needed to run was the unpaved, half-mile drive that led to our house. In my father's estimation, this undertaking, so monumental it could've kept the local Teamsters union busy for a week, was perfect for a pre-teen boy to tackle by himself at the going feudal wage of $1.35 an hour.

As with many things, the first time was the most memorable. It was four degrees Fahrenheit when my father took me outside and showed me where to start. He said he had army reserve weapons training that day and would be gone from 7:30 a.m. until 4:30 p.m., but expected me to be finished by the time he got home. Determined to turn me into a lawyer, doctor or banker, he wanted to show me how hard it was to work with your hands instead of your head.

With a sledgehammer in my gloved grip and brutally cold wind making its way through every fiber of my down jacket, I stepped awkwardly from our frozen front lawn into the thick brush surrounding it, where rolled-up fencing and the seven foot metal stakes needed to hold the barricade up lay buried from the year before. Digging these steel strips out from the lifeless, brown overgrowth that covered them, I prepared for the first part of the job; pounding one into the Earth every ten feet for the full half mile distance.

My first problem was my height. I was shorter than the stakes and thus had no leverage every time I lifted the sledgehammer above my shoulders and swung it down toward the desired point of impact, which sat a foot and a half above my head. As a result, each of my hits, even when direct, was ineffective and did little to dent the ground, which coincidentally was my second problem. It was hard as concrete. Typically, a snow fence is put up in September or October before the first frost, but it was November now and the dirt was almost impenetrable.

As I struggled mightily over the next hour to get one and then two stakes planted; muscling them into the soil like square pegs in round holes, a swirling blizzard kicked up and engulfed me, making my mission increasingly objectionable. Staring off into the storm down the now-obscured half mile drive and contemplating the circumstances I found myself in, I decided to do what any sane person would do in the same situation. I went inside and subcontracted out the job.

Bribing my friends over the phone with a promise of food and cash, I soon had a coterie of laborers ideally suited for the effort required. Steve Danesi was tall so I put him to work pounding stakes; something he had a real knack for as it turned out. Paul Wood was strong so I enlisted him to unroll the fencing through the weed-choked terrain. And Chris Pardi had tiny hands which were just right for the type of intricate wiring work needed to hold the fencing to the stakes. They were a perfect threesome.

In the meantime, I assumed an oversight role, attending to payroll and benefits issues from a perch inside the house. A lovely picture window allowed me to keep a close eye on the staff to make sure corners weren't being cut. I

How to Raise a Good Kid

told them my trust but verify approach was nothing they should take personally, and they seemed to understand that someone had to wear the black hat of management.

When my father walked in the door from army training at 5:00 p.m. and saw the four of us eating pizza and drinking hot chocolate at the kitchen table, he was not pleased.

"What the hell's going on here?" he asked.

"Just a business dinner, Dad," I said. "It's deductible. You remember my colleagues Steve, Paul and Chris, right?" I asked.

"Your colleagues? Why isn't the fence finished?" he fumed.

"Well, we ran into some weather difficulties and the guys got a bit hungry halfway down the road so I gave them a break. It's Miller time," I said.

"I told you I wanted the fence finished today," he said.

"I know that and I'm not going to lie. We're a little behind schedule and a little over budget, but the good news is the guys are doing a top notch job and they're going to finish it up no later than noon tomorrow," I said.

"This wasn't their job to do," my father said. "It was yours."

In the years that followed, my father made sure that I mowed my share of lawns, shoveled my share of snow and raked my share of gravel. In the process, I learned the lessons he hoped I would about hard work, the difficulty of manual labor, the importance of staying in school and the inherent benefits of making your living with your head instead of your hands. But of all the lessons I learned, none stuck with me more than the lesson I learned from my first experience with the snow fence: it's good to be the boss.

11
Persistence

Take Me Out of the Ball Game

The late Judah Folkman, a prominent cancer researcher, frequently spoke to his Harvard students about the fine line between persistence and obstinacy when pursuing a particular research pathway and its accompanying hypotheses. His question: how long do you continue to travel in the same direction when you encounter repeated failures along the way? Not knowing when to quit was something he struggled with his whole career.

I was made aware of Dr. Folkman by a friend who studied under him and told me of his death. I'm sorry that we never met because I believe I could have offered him some valuable insight by sharing a brief history of my years in little league baseball. Although Dr. Folkman focused on the problems encountered by medical researchers, he faced a dilemma that's recognizable to anyone who's ever had a dream.

My dream was to be the first baseman for the world champion Cincinnati Reds. The year was 1975 and playing baseball was more than just a rite of passage for every boy. It was a way of life and, to a large extent, a defining activity. Your self-esteem was comprised of four basic elements: your position (a hierarchy where playing right field was at the bottom and meant you were pretty much useless), your team's won-loss record, your place in the batting order and, most important, your batting average.

My journey toward professional baseball immortality began at age eight when my parents signed me up for tee-ball league and I was assigned to play for Home Federal, a local savings bank and our sponsor. Unhappy the team's colors were orange and white instead of red and white like my heroes, I was consoled by my father who said the bank's long-term CD rates were attractive and that I should be proud to represent the institution.

Everything got off to a wonderful start. I advised our coach, Mr. Tyler, that I should be the team's first baseman since I was left-handed. As I explained to him, the results of the research I'd conducted in the school library showed that it was a natural advantage to have a southpaw in this position due to the superior throwing angles it created. Seemingly dumbfounded by my thoroughness and clearly impressed I'd found time to complete the study given my hectic fourth-grade schedule, Mr. Tyler acquiesced.

After securing a premier position, I turned my attention to my batting. With above-average eye-hand coordination, I was made for tee-ball, which required nothing more of me than to smash a stationary baseball off a

How to Raise a Good Kid

three-foot high upright rubber cylinder. Batting third in the line-up, I was successful more than half the time resulting in a final average of .508; 100 points higher than the best average ever recorded in the major leagues. And though the team disappointed by finishing in second place after winning only four of its five games, I felt confident in my hypothesis that I was headed for the bigs.

The next year, I graduated to the nine-year old division and joined a team sponsored by Phoenix Mutual, an insurance company with lousy yellow and white uniforms but terrific annuity products. Mr. Tyler was my coach again and immediately installed me at first base having remembered my research.

The nine-year old division was fast-pitch, meaning no more tees, but this was a misnomer because nobody could throw very hard, and the resulting emphasis on accuracy over the plate created a batter's paradise. Once again, I feasted on the pitching and posted a .354 batting average as our team went undefeated and won the league championship. With Kool-Aid flowing like champagne, these heady days only got headier as I was named to the league all-star team. I was on top of the baseball world and my experiment, conducted to confirm my future employment with the Cincinnati Reds, was yielding all the right results.

Unfortunately, then came ten, the age when all boys in my town's little league program were required to try-out for the majors, a division that housed kids for three years up through age twelve. Following try-outs, there was a draft, and those who were selected joined the major league while those who weren't selected were cast into purgatory; also known as the minors, a home for the athletically challenged.

Rain on the day of try-outs forced everyone inside the high school gym where each prospect was allowed the opportunity to demonstrate his ability to field, hit and run quickly around orange cones. I left satisfied; convinced my talent had shone through, and a week later, the day of the draft, I waited by the telephone for good news. League officials told us that selections for the majors would be made in rounds lasting from noon until 5:00 p.m. and that we would be called sometime between those hours if we were chosen.

At 4:30 p.m., I still had not received a call.

"Do you think they're going to call, Dad?" I asked.

He looked conflicted, like he wasn't sure what to say given my decreasing odds.

"Sure, they will," he said.

"Did you give them the right phone number?" I asked.

"Yes, they've got it."

The clock ticked by until it was 4:55 p.m. and I decided to go out in the backyard and contemplate my soon-to-be altered life as an outcast. Dejectedly walking the perimeter of our freshly-cut lawn, I was startled when my father called out from our porch a few minutes later.

"You made it!" he shouted.

"I did?" I ran toward him, beaming broadly.

"Yes. You were drafted by Community Savings Bank," he said.

"Really? That's great! What are their colors?" I inquired.

"Blue and white, but they've got very reasonable mortgage rates," he said.

"Awesome!" I replied.

That night, when the excitement subsided and I finally calmed down, I wondered why it took so long

How to Raise a Good Kid

for me to be drafted. Although I was thrilled to be headed up to the majors, knowing I'd been one of the last players selected made me uncertain about my skills for the first time. Instead of a success, the draft felt like a setback. Wasn't I as good as I thought? That question would be answered over the coming season.

Community Savings Bank was the New York Yankees of the league with a history of great players, great teams and championship seasons. Our coach, Mr. Borroff, stressed to us that we were being entrusted with the team's historic legacy and that we had a responsibility to uphold its tradition of winning. Losing and losers would not be tolerated under any circumstances. Of course, he wanted us to have fun, too.

I was ready to do my part and approached every practice with the ferocity of a tiger tearing into a gazelle. My goal was to out hit, out field and out hustle every player on the team. But no matter how hard I worked, I couldn't overcome the limitations of being a small ten-year old competing against large twelve-year olds, and when positions were assigned, I was left standing out in right field; no longer a first baseman.

The indignities didn't end there. Under league rules, every player had to play at least two innings in the field every game but could be benched after that requirement was met. Never playing more than two innings, I quickly realized I was someone Coach Borroff had to insert into each game against his will; repeatedly strategizing as to when I would do the least damage. Standing briefly in right field and batting eighth, I found consolation in the team's ongoing undefeated record.

At the plate, where I batted once or, at most, twice

per game, I was determined to make an impact and I did — sort of. Unlike the nine-year olds I'd faced, the twelve-year old pitchers tended to be overgrown Eastern European types with facial hair who could throw bullets but had little control and, as a result, I began to get beaned with some frequency. Although taking pitches in my ribs or head often left me lying flat on my back with a team of medical specialists and my parents gathered around, it also got me on base which pleased Coach Borroff. Occasionally I would draw a walk, hit a squibber or even drive the ball out of the infield, but my major contribution was getting hit by pitches.

At the end of the season, Community Savings Bank was the league champion and we gathered for a team banquet at a local party house. I had come to accept my role on the team. I may not have been an all-star, but I felt I was a valuable contributor. In my mind, I thought there was a good possibility I would be recognized with an award at the banquet. I wasn't sure what, but perhaps most valuable rookie, most improved player or some kind of plaque designating me the team sparkplug. I believed this kind of affirmation would be enough to keep me on track toward playing professionally.

Over the next three hours as we ate pizza and cake, speeches were made and awards were handed out, but my name was never mentioned. We each received a trophy for our league championship and, in the absence of anything else; I clung to it as the banquet began to wind down.

Just then, I saw Coach Borroff making his way across the floor toward me. Here it comes, I thought. He wants to personally thank me for my contributions. Very classy move. Coach Borroff reached me and handed me

How to Raise a Good Kid

a folded piece of paper. "I want you to have this," he said, walking off. I was touched. He had taken the time to write me a note. Anxious to see what he'd written, I opened it up and stared down at the text. Batting Average — .000 was all it said.

With my eyes watering, I moved toward the door avoiding eye contact with everyone. In all my figuring, it had never occurred to me that I failed to register an actual hit the entire season. I hadn't contributed at all to the team's championship. I was a total zero. This wasn't a setback to my dream. It was the complete annihilation of it.

Like the kind of dilemma Dr. Folkman warned his fellow medical researchers about, it was one of those instances where the mere act of continuing threatened to turn the admirable quality of persistence into the less desirable one of obstinacy. I had every reason to quit playing baseball, but I didn't. If I had given up then, I believe it would have permanently changed me and not for the better. Surrendering to this devastating event and its corresponding effect on my ego would have left me defenseless against future defeats and less willing to engage in the act of reaching for something beyond my likely grasp.

Instead, I returned the next year to play for Community Savings Bank as an 11-year old. By then, I knew I was not headed for the Cincinnati Reds and a professional career, but I wanted to test my new hypothesis; one that posited I would feel satisfied if I showed determination and better results, and that doing so was important for its own sake.

That season, I was not an all-star, but I played more, batted a respectable .286 and celebrated when the team won yet another league title. After that, I promptly quit the sport, took up tennis and put Wimbledon in my sights. I think Dr. Folkman would have been proud.

12
Self-Determination

Requiem for a Team

On November 5, 1972, my father took me to my first football game. Following our move to western New York a few years before, he had gone native — adopting the Buffalo Bills as his team — and was now ready to initiate me into the same rooting fraternity. Fathers didn't talk about bonding experiences back then and mine was no exception, but that was clearly what he had in mind: father and son; side by side; cheering on the home team together.

Our outing got off to a great start. During the hour long drive to Buffalo, my father regaled me with stories of the team's history, particularly its two American Football League championships earned in 1964 and 1965. He wanted me to know that the Bills were winners and that those who supported them could lay claim to the same mantle. I nodded dutifully and made a beeline for the bag of sandwiches my mother had prepared for us; chewing contentedly on bologna and cheese as we drove onward.

A little ways down the road, my father tuned in the AM sports radio station that covered the team. I knew I was about to witness something vitally important from listening to his stories, but the serious tone of the announcers as they discussed the Bills various offensive and defensive schemes convinced me that this was much more than a football game; it was a matter of life and death. As the radio jocks broke down the Bills injury report, it occurred to me that someone might be killed on the field that day, but if the Bills won it would all be worth it.

With my soul already stirring, it surged when, a short time later, a colossus of concrete appeared before us; rising in the distance like a secret city only the blessed could enter.

"There it is, son. The Ol' Rockpile," he said, referring to Buffalo's War Memorial Stadium by its nickname. "For my money, there's no better place to take in a ball game."

On this count, I accepted my father at his word. Although a writer once quipped that the war honored by Buffalo's War Memorial must have taken place within its walls given its catastrophic appearance, five-year old little boys don't notice such things. Plus, I'd never been to another stadium and I was awed by its size and scope as well as the pageantry that accompanied the event.

"Now, we're going to tailgate, son," my father said, having parked in lot H with thousands of other fans and opened the back door of our station wagon horizontally.

"We are? What's a tailgate?" I asked.

"It's a great and uniquely American tradition. Patriotic people from far and wide come stand together in a parking lot to grill Polish sausage and drink beer. It's what Thomas Jefferson envisioned when he wrote the Bill of Rights."

"Did our founders tailgate?"

"Well, maybe not quite like this, but they had their own version with horses."

Until then, I never realized how integral eating and drinking were to football. I learned that some of the tailgaters waited until halftime before heading into the stadium and that some never headed in at all. It was truly a remarkable game.

Leaving our blacktop brethren behind after stuffing ourselves with sausage, my father and I headed through the awaiting security gates just before kick-off.

"Get your Bills pennants and programs, here," a vendor shouted as we walked up a ramp and caught a full view of the field.

"Do you want a pennant?" my father asked.

"Sure," I said, excitedly grabbing the wooden stick attached to it from the vendor's hand.

"What do you say?" my father asked.

"Thanks," I replied.

"How about a program?" he asked.

"Yes, please."

My father's master plan to make me a Bills fan was coming together. He had me just where he wanted me; happily ensconced in row 48 with my pennant and program. His dream was so close he could touch it; like the steaming pile of nachos soon placed on my lap.

Unfortunately, as with many dreams, this one began to go awry. It's difficult to conduct an autopsy with confidence given the passage of time, but the beginning of the end may have started with the pennant.

It was subtle as a slight breeze, but I noticed something was wrong with the buffalo depicted on the pennant.

"There's something wrong with this buffalo, Dad," I said, pointing to the animal sitting squarely in the center of the Bills helmet on my new prize possession.

"What?" my father asked.

"He looks sick," I said. "See his face."

"No, he's not sick. He's just determined. That's a look of determination."

"Why's his head down?" I asked. "Is he going to throw up?"

Buffalo's forlorn logo at the time was a bison standing still while staring down at his two front hoofs. Far from appearing ferocious, the animal looked like it was in line at a slaughterhouse.

"No, the buffalo's not going to throw up," my father said. "He's just gathering his thoughts before he attacks."

"Oh," I said, still skeptical that the buffalo on my pennant was Grade A meat.

Turning my attention to the program, I began to discover some unnerving facts about the Bills starting with their current record of two wins and six losses on the season. In contrast, their opponent, the Miami Dolphins, had a perfect record through eight games.

"The Dolphins are undefeated," I announced.

"It won't last," my father assured me. "They haven't played anyone yet," he said, easily dismissing a third of the league's teams as nobodies.

"Dad, what's the Super Bowl?"

"It's the last game of the year when the two best teams play each other and the winner is crowned world champion."

"Did you know the Dolphins were in the Super Bowl last year?" I asked.

"Yes, I knew that. They got beat by the Cowboys 24 to 3."

"Have the Bills ever been to the Super Bowl?" I asked.

"Not yet. But I guarantee you they will be very soon."

Undaunted by my blitz of inquiries, my father still had a good chance to turn me into a Bills fan. All he needed was the team and its star, O.J. Simpson, a.k.a The Juice, to play well. And as the crowd came alive for the Bills first offensive possession, hope, chants and beer breath filled the cold Buffalo air.

"Let's Go Buff-a-Lo! Let's Go Buff-a-Lo! Let's Go Buff-a-Lo!"

The masses wanted blood or a touchdown and preferably both. Everyone in the Ol' Rockpile knew what was coming next. The Bills were going to try to turn The Juice loose.

"Juice! Juice! Juice!" The rabble was roused.

The Bills ran O.J. to the right. They ran him to the left. They ran him straight up the middle. Each time the Dolphin defense held.

"Booooooooooooo!"

Patience was not a virtue to the average Bills fan nor was tolerance so when the Dolphins scored first on a 33-yard field goal from Garo Yepremian, a kicker born in Cyprus, the stadium shook with displeasure and ethnic slurs.

"Go back to China, you commie," a man in the row behind us barked.

Geopolitical undercurrents notwithstanding, I was learning new things by the moment as the lead changed hands several times and the excitement at the Ol'

Rockpile built. For instance, after hearing a dozen different people question every penalty that went against the Bills; punctuating their remarks with the phrase, "What are you blind, ref?" or a more colorful version thereof, I concluded that football spectators knew more about the rules of the game than the referees; some of whom apparently suffered from visual impairment. What a sport!

Entering the fourth quarter, the score stood at 23-16 in the Dolphins' favor, but my father predicted a Buffalo victory.

"This is where they're going to do it, son," my father said. "The fourth quarter belongs to the Bills."

Although the program indicated the Bills had been outscored in the fourth quarter in every game but one that season, I didn't have the heart to tell him as he joined the growing chorus.

"Let's Go Buff-a-Lo! Let's Go Buff-a-Lo! Let's Go Buff-a-Lo!"

With only a touchdown separating the teams, the true believers had reason to hope. There was still time for The Juice to get loose and spoil the Dolphins perfect season. There was still time for me to become a Bills fan.

The football gods, however, weren't smiling. And when Mercury Morris scored on a 4-yard run; thereby extending the Dolphins lead to 30-16, my father's dream officially expired.

The Dolphins beat the Bills that day and would go on to complete what remains the only undefeated season in professional football history; winning the Super Bowl over the Washington Redskins. They would also win the Super Bowl the next year; cementing my place in the team's fandom for life. In contrast, the Bills would finish the year with 4 wins and 10 losses, and wouldn't beat the Dolphins until 1980.

Looking back, my father's dream never stood a chance. Was it the pennant or the program or the fact the Dolphins were on the cusp of football history? Probably a combination of all three but I'll never know for sure. Perhaps I was subconsciously separating from him; trying to establish my own identity in the middle of Bills country.

Today, my father still roots for the Bills and I still root for the Dolphins. We make a small bet with each other every time they play, and both notoriously forget to pay if our team loses. After all these years, it's remarkable how much we have in common.

13
Necessary Rites of Passage

King of the Mall

There were no mean streets to roam where I grew up. My friends and I had no dark alleys to explore or abandoned warehouses to investigate. We didn't have a dangerous part of town or even a Hooters. Instead, we had the mall; an artificially-lit retail paradise that doubled as our proving ground.

Who we were proving ourselves to was a mystery. As a group of eleven-year old suburban punks (and I say that affectionately), we wanted for little except more independence, a bit of danger and some extra time with our brand new discovery — girls. The mall provided all three plus a Burger King, so we couldn't visit often enough.

Our mall was called Eastview and it was built when the trend toward massive indoor shopping centers was in its infancy. Many of its stores were not part of national chains, but were independently owned by local entrepreneurs. There was no Supercuts or Fantastic Sam's. There was only Gino's; where you could peruse the latest Playboy while Gino cut your hair to the sound of Italian opera songs. There was no Gap or Banana Republic. There was only The Shed House; where piles of blue jeans lined the walls of a faux shack that looked like something Jed Clampett might have built. We didn't have Nordstrom's and its wide variety of luxury goods. We had The Nomad and its wide variety of bowls, bongs, knives and rolling papers; the perfect place for impressionable sixth graders. These stores and others like them gave Eastview its own unique personality and spirit, and made each visit an exciting adventure.

Every weekend, usually on a Saturday afternoon, a group of us would meet at Eastview and stay as long as our parents allowed or until the mall closed. In the intervening hours, we experienced the closest thing to freedom that we'd ever known. Walking the behemoth's green-carpeted corridors, we were the kings of all we surveyed; convinced that those left in our wake were not just impressed by our style, our haircuts and our swagger, but permanently transformed. Nobody in the history of mankind had ever been or would ever be as cool as us. This much was certain.

What made the mall so intoxicating were the limitless opportunities it presented. Hankering for a free sample of beefsteak or cheese at Hickory Farms? Done. Need a mug that says World's Greatest Mom? Just walk into Lock, Stock and Barrel. Want to smell something funky? Let's go down to Pampered Pets.

Eastview was akin to a casino; a temperature-controlled, clock-free environment designed by management to remove every dollar from your pocket before you left. And it worked. Typically armed with $15 a piece, we would spend it all in a fairly predictable pattern — $6.99 plus tax on a KISS album at Record Theatre; another $4.00 or so on food and a Coke at Burger King; and whatever was left on something from Spencer's Gifts.

No trip to Eastview was complete without a visit to Spencer's; a place we revered as the mall's Mecca. It was as if someone had designed a store just for us; every inch of it covered with things we desired. Where else in the world could you find a Lava Lamp, a can of Fart Spray and a poster of Adrienne Barbeau in a purple negligee all in the same aisle? No place I'd ever been before. It was heaven on Earth and we spent hours there admiring the merchandise.

But the best thing about going to Eastview was the anticipation we felt entering its doors. Without computers, cell phones, text messages, Twitter and the like, we came to the mall to socialize with friends and more important, the opposite sex. It wasn't a question of if we'd see girls we knew; it was only a question of which ones. And to our great benefit, we weren't hidden away in our bedrooms updating our MySpace or Facebook pages. Instead, we were out in the world, strutting our stuff down Eastview's ramparts and looking for a live connection.

Nothing matched the thrill of seeing the girl you liked — the one you'd stolen glances of at school — walking toward you. She might be with friends or her mother but, either way; you were forced to stand your ground, act nonchalantly and fight the overwhelming urge to duck into Radio Shack. After all, your fellow mall kings were watching and you had to be cool. Your interaction with her was invariably brief, but you'd spend the rest of the weekend silently analyzing everything she said while assuring your friends you weren't interested in her at all. Then, when Monday came and classes resumed, you'd look for her everywhere you went; in the hallways, the gym, the cafeteria — waiting for a moment when you might catch eyes.

After many years away, I moved back to my hometown this summer but I don't go to Eastview often. I hate parking lots and crowds so most of my shopping is done online. When I do go, it depresses me. It's not the changes to the mall since I left that have ruined the experience. I can live with the fact that my childhood stomping ground has lost its original charm and become interchangeable with any other mall. What bothers me much more and what I can't live with is the fact that I don't know anyone there anymore. When I walk around Eastview today, I feel like a complete stranger; miles away from the king I was long ago. All my friends have moved away; their parents dead or retired to places unknown. The girls I knew have all grown up, gotten married and left the area. Seeing a familiar face or two used to be a guarantee. Now it's a long shot. I look for friendly faces but I see none. I look for The Nomad and The Shed House and Gino's, but they're gone. Even Spencer's brings no relief; its gifts more reflective of today's coarser tone and devoid of the innocence I remember. It's as if all the wires that once connected me to this place are down.

All, however, is not lost. The melancholy I feel is

certainly not fatal, and though I'm no longer a king of the mall and never will be again, I can see a day when my feelings about going there may change. Now that I have a son and have permanently returned, it won't be long until I'm dropping him off at Eastview and watching him set off on his own adventure. And, perhaps, with the passage of time, the anonymity and rootlessness I currently feel when I visit Eastview will fade away as I meet more people and integrate back into my old community. Maybe, someday soon, I'll start seeing faces that I know once again and, for a few seconds, I'll remember what it's like to be a king of the mall.

14
The Meaning of Tradition

Uncle Frank

The trip took nine hours each way give or take a few minutes. Every year, around 4:00 p.m. the day before Thanksgiving, after my mother finished her duties teaching third grade, we piled into our packed station wagon and headed for my Uncle Frank's house in Connecticut. Preparing to drive late into the night, my father turned the back seat of the car into a bed where my sister and I would eventually fall asleep to the dull, rhythmic thumping of wheels rolling over pavement. To me, it always seemed like a long way to travel for a single meal. But my father said going to Frank's was a family tradition and, until I was adopted by a new set of parents, it was not an optional activity.

Uncle Frank was my grandfather's only brother and, following my grandfather's death in 1964, he became a father figure for my dad. My father had gone to Frank's house for Thanksgiving every year since he was a young boy and he wanted his children to have the same experience. He also wanted us to get to know Frank who possessed a host of qualities my father admired. What those qualities were escaped me at first. All I saw during my first few visits was that Frank had several hairs growing out of his nose; wasn't much for small talk; and had a large collection of guns, which he displayed in two large cases made of wood and glass in his living room. With time, I would come to learn this was all part of his charm.

Frank was completely self-reliant. A widowed architect and veteran, he had designed and built a beautiful home on a bluff overlooking the Atlantic Ocean in the small town of Noank. Frank did all his own cooking, cleaning and repair work, and was an avid hunter. The turkey we ate was always one he'd shot, skinned, stuffed and seasoned before placing it in the oven. He was like Julia Child with a rifle.

Frank was also a patriot with a zero tolerance policy for Nazis, Communists and pansies. When World War II broke out, Frank immediately signed up for military service, leaving behind both his career and family; an ordinary act until you consider that he was 42 years old at the time. He spent the next four years as a gunnery sergeant, helping in his own small way to defeat Hitler. And though he was convinced that Nazism and its followers had been eradicated, he still saw Communists at every turn; mostly in the stores, restaurants and community theatres dotting the Connecticut coastline. Due to this threat, Uncle Frank understood the need to stay heavily armed and to keep his extended family

How to Raise a Good Kid

heavily armed. My birthday gift every year was a new camouflage jacket and a box of shotgun shells; items he presented to me at Thanksgiving even though I was born in August. As for pansies, Frank's feelers went up any time he saw me carrying around a stuffed animal. In his mind, this was a warning sign that I was on the wrong path and an event that invariably required my father to provide assurance to Frank that I played tackle football and enjoyed it.

Frank dressed in a serious manner. Men of his generation believed that it was important to present themselves to the world in the best possible way. Growing up at a time when Brooks Brothers set the standard for fine clothing, he always looked like he'd just stepped out of their store with perfectly tailored pants, newly-shined shoes and an orderly-shaped bowtie affixed around his neck. My grandfather had been the same way and my father emulated both of them. Peeking into Frank's closet, I was certain I'd never met anyone with more tweed jackets.

Frank didn't suffer fools gladly; an inconvenient trait given that our family contained its share, none more prominent than Frank's son, Henry. Frank wanted Henry to pursue a profession but Henry had other ideas and decided to open a small wooden toy factory where he claimed to have whittled the world's smallest violin. Henry usually smelled like a combination of sawdust and Bushmills Irish Whiskey, but he was tremendously talented and good-spirited as well as notorious for visiting the kid's table to entertain us by running his finger through the candle flame. Unfortunately, Frank considered him a disappointment and often treated him as such, creating a tension that even a child could perceive.

Like all those before and after him, Frank was a product of his times and a man with strengths and flaws. His father, a New York City Court judge, was a stern man with high expectations for his children and it would have been difficult, if not impossible, for Frank to be different. Frank spent his youth away at boarding school and had a relationship with his parents that was more distant and formal than those seen in modern parenthood. And though this was not unusual for his day and age, it made it hard for him to show the kind of affection one associates with love. Frank was a man who met you with a handshake not a hug.

Each trip to Connecticut, however, taught me that Frank was much more than a gruff curmudgeon with a house full of guns. Although he had strong reservations about the toy business, he invested in Henry's company and spent time every week looking after Henry's son, Sean. I also learned that, prior to becoming a widower, Frank had tended patiently and without complaint to his ailing wife, my late Aunt Marion, who suffered from crippling arthritis and was eventually bed bound. And there was no question he took genuine pleasure hosting our entire extended family for Thanksgiving. There was an unmistakable look of satisfaction on his face as he welcomed you into his immaculate home full of antiques, hardwood floors and oriental rugs.

For better or worse, Frank was our family's patriarch, its oldest living member and the keeper of its history. So when we put on our jackets and ties, and ate and drank at a table Frank set using silverware passed down by prior generations, we were connecting with and honoring, in a small but significant way, the lineage of O'Dwyer's

— the righteous, the rogues and the renegades — who came from Ireland to make a life in America. The same stories were told year after year about late grandparents and great-grandparents and for a very brief moment in time they came alive and joined us in the room.

Going to Frank's had always been important to my father. It was a chance for him to spend a day or two with someone who knew his father intimately well and could remind him of all the things he loved about his own dad. But what surprised me was how important going to Frank's became for me, my sister and my cousins. Despite its short duration, the time spent there and the impressions it left were monumental. It gave us a strong sense of who we were and where we came from, and made us feel part of something continuous, solid and bigger than the small world we inhabited from day to day.

Uncle Frank died when I was sixteen and for several years we stopped getting together as an extended family for Thanksgiving. His death coincided with a difficult period of change which saw our clan experience the full spectrum of problems life affords both personal and professional. Making matters worse, Frank's son, my Uncle Henry, died during this time, forcing the sale of the home in Noank and further splintering us as a group. Somehow, without Frank, we forgot about the enjoyment we derived from our annual pilgrimage to Connecticut and entered a period in the wilderness with everyone unhappily scattered across the country at holiday time.

Then, in 1989, my sister got married; bringing everyone together once more. Not long after, my parents resurrected the tradition of Thanksgiving by hosting everyone at their home. For twenty years now, we've reunited annually and it has become an increasingly meaningful occasion for all those who attend. The family has grown with spouses and children and friends who come from near and far. The men wear jackets and ties. The women wear dresses. Laughter is abundant. And we tell the same stories; ones we never tire of hearing; especially ones about our dear old Uncle Frank.

15
Adapting to Change

No Place Like Home

"I've got exciting news," my father said, arriving home from work. "We're going to Europe this summer."

Europe? Wow. My mind took off as I imagined all the places we'd see. London — Paris — Rome — The Great Wall of China. I was ready for my first trip abroad and the adventure of a lifetime. This was a monumental announcement for lots of reasons but mostly because my family was not part of the jet set; far from it. My parents' idea of a great vacation was cramming everyone into our Ford Country Squire station wagon and driving twelve hours in the rain to Nova Scotia. At ten-years of age, I'd never been on a plane, but that streak was about to end.

"This is so cool. When do we leave?" I asked, bouncing around like a rubber ball next to my father.

"I'm only taking Mom," he said, matter-of-factly.

"Dad, that's not funny."

"I'm sorry, but I can't take you. You're going to stay with the Brennan's. I've already talked to them."

"But, Dad, I want to go with you."

"Next time. This is a military trip."

"Military?" I asked, anxiously.

"Yes. To Germany."

I gulped. Now this was getting serious.

"Are you going to war, Dad?"

"No, I'm not going to war. I'm going to a NATO conference," he said. "I've been asked to serve as a representative of the U.S. Army at the annual meeting in Bonn."

"Will there be Nazis there?"

"No. No Nazis."

Assured that the biggest risk to my parents while in Germany would be a bad piece of wiener schnitzel, I relaxed and neglected to question the month of leisure travel my father was tacking on to their time at the conference. It was hard to accept at first that my parents would want to spend a day let alone five weeks without me, but I had to face reality. While they traipsed around Europe nibbling on scones at outdoor cafes, I would have to fend for myself in a strange new environment.

For me, this meant bunking at the Brennan's. Long-time social friends of my parents with three kids around my age, the Brennan's kindly agreed to take me in for the summer and treat me as one of their own; a prospect that seemed harmless on its face but proved sobering in practice. I'd never spent more than a week away from my parents and was a little afraid of what might happen if I did. Although it's easy to take your family for granted after

How to Raise a Good Kid

years inside the comfortable confines of your home and usual routine, I had no idea how guilty I was of this crime.

As with most catastrophes, there were ominous signs from the start. After saying goodbye to my parents and chasing after their car in tears as they drove off, I returned to learn I'd be sharing a bedroom with Kevin, the Brennan's oldest son; a bully who specialized in purple nurples, titty twisters and Indian rug burns. Kevin wasn't happy about the arrangement and expressed his heartfelt desire to kill me as we climbed the stairs to deposit my suitcase. I told him I hoped we could make the best of it and maybe even become friends at which point he threatened to give me an atomic wedgie.

Once inside his bedroom, I figured the key to survival would be compliments and small talk; so I praised his Oakland Raiders trash can and struck up a conversation about the U.S. flag standing in the corner.

"Hey, that's a great flag," I said.

"It's American," he announced.

"Uh . . . yeah . . . I can see that."

Worried my glib tone might offend, I nervously offered up some trivia to diffuse any powder keg I'd lit.

"Did you know the flag has 13 stripes for the original 13 colonies and 50 stars; one for each state in the union?"

"I guess they need to change it now that there's 53 states," Kevin said.

"What do you mean? There aren't 53 states," I said.

"Yes, there are!"

"No, there aren't," I said.

"Yes there are! You wanna die?"

Kevin moved closer to intimidate me; his head the color of a red hot tamale. I should've backed off given his immense size advantage and obvious anger issues but, with my father off fighting the Germans, I was feeling particularly patriotic and brave.

"Let's ask your dad," I said, seeking a third party arbitrator in hopes of avoiding a purple nurple, death or worse.

"Fine," Kevin huffed.

When Mr. Brennan arrived, I fully expected him to set his son straight but I soon learned that Kevin had the home field advantage. Upon learning the nature of our dispute, Mr. Brennan said that although there were fifty states, the U.S. also had at least three territories that he knew of including Puerto Rico, Guam, and American Samoa; so, in effect, we were both right. Naturally, Kevin declared victory and I spent the rest of the evening stewing over this injustice. Clearly, the Brennan's hadn't been washing the pesticide off their fruit.

Nevertheless, when morning came, I decided to forget about the prior night's disappointment and make a good faith effort at fitting in with the Brennan family. I would be there for the foreseeable future so I needed to make it work. Adopting a positive attitude as I got dressed, I anticipated the wonderful smells that would soon wend their way upstairs; alerting me to the presence of pancakes and bacon, my favorites. Regrettably, those smells never arrived. Instead, only my sense of hearing was employed as Mrs. Brennan called us down to breakfast like a hyena whose foot was caught in a bear trap.

"BREKFASSSSSST!"

Tramping down the stairs behind Kevin and his siblings Mary-Pat and Matthew, I took my seat at the kitchen table and tried to blend in; still hoping for the best. Although there were no pancakes, waffles, eggs or breakfast meats, there was cereal. And after slogging through a bowl of Grape Nuts (Kevin's therapist had banned his use of Frosted Flakes and the like), I indulged in a piece of warm toast, one of life's true comfort foods. This isn't so bad, I thought, trying to compensate for the absence of my mother's cooking. Closing my eyes and savoring its buttery goodness, I thought of my parents far away; sitting in a foxhole or perhaps the lobby of a small hotel. I missed them terribly.

Awaking from my reverie, I cleared my dishes as I'd been taught and decided to wash my hands in the kitchen sink for good measure. My mother had reminded me several times to use my best manners and I didn't want to let her down. Unfortunately, after drying my hands on a paper towel and discarding it in the trash bin under the sink, I abruptly learned that proper etiquette can vary from family to family.

"What are you doing?" Mrs. Brennan asked me in an accusatory voice; a crazed look on her face.

"Just washing my hands," I said, holding them up in the air for inspection.

"I'm talking about the paper towel," Mrs. Brennan continued, clearly annoyed.

Standing by the sink and looking back at the cabinet that housed the trash, I searched my brain in a futile attempt to figure out what I'd done wrong.

"We don't just throw those out," Mrs. Brennan said.

"We don't?" I asked.

"No, we don't," she said.

"Are you stupid?" Kevin called out from the breakfast table.

"No, I'm not stupid," I said, waiting for Mrs. Brennan to admonish her son for use of such language.

"Now, I have no idea what goes on in your house, but here we re-use our paper towels," Mrs. Brennan said, insinuating my entire family was profligate in its ways.

"Oh," I said, unsure of how to react.

Mrs. Brennan retrieved my damp paper towel from the garbage and instructed me to follow her into the laundry room.

"See this," she said, pointing to a small wooden rack standing on top of the dryer. "This is where we hang our paper towels to dry. And this is where you will hang your paper towels to dry."

Hanging paper towels to dry was the dumbest thing I'd ever heard of in my life; not to mention the grossest, but Mrs. Brennan's words had a fervor that frightened me and made me think twice about expressing my opinion. It was all academic because, within seconds, she pushed me further into the Dickensian nightmare from which I couldn't wake.

"And while we're on the subject . . . ," she said, leading me back into the kitchen, "you will get one glass to use all day."

"I'm not sure I understand."

"See your juice glass?" she asked, picking it off the table. "Once you're done with it, you will rinse it out and leave it by the sink. Later, if you want a glass of water or milk or soda pop, you will use the same glass."

"All of that in the same glass?" I asked, disbelieving.

"Yes. All in the same glass."

"What about paper cups?" I asked, hoping there was an exception to the rule.

"We don't use paper cups in this house," Mrs. Brennan said.

How to Raise a Good Kid 103

"Are you stupid?" Kevin called out again. "We don't use paper cups."

"That's enough, Kevin," Mrs. Brennan said.

My mild fear transformed immediately into terror. What had my parents done? How could they have left me with these maniacs? They weren't kind. They weren't stable. And they weren't normal. They were a bunch of one-cup using, paper towel hanging, 53-state flagging freaks; and I was stuck with them.

Like a soldier retreating from enemy fire, I tried to escape but it was impossible. At every turn, I confronted the fact the Brennan's did everything differently than my family. They drank Kool-Aid. We drank Hi-C. They ate Skippy. We ate Jif. They played differently. They prayed differently. TV was forbidden and dessert was fruit. I was an alien on a distant planet and I longed for my own home, where paper towels flowed freely, cups were plentiful and sandwiches were cut in half instead of in fours. Staring into this dark abyss, I made survival my only goal.

And then, just when I thought even that modest goal was in doubt, the oddest thing happened. Days began to pass and I began to adjust to my new living conditions. Kevin was still a Neanderthal but Matthew wasn't, and when the three of us hung out, making fun of each other mercilessly in the process, I understood for the first time what it would be like to have brothers; an experience I enjoyed. We rode bikes everywhere and spent most of the next few weeks unsupervised; flaunting our independence and courting the kind of danger that's easy to flee. We also rode skateboards, something I'd never done before, and made a pilgrimage each day to Abbott's for frozen custard, a local specialty to which I developed an addiction. As long as we came home by dinner, the Brennan's left us alone; a very pleasant surprise to me.

Under their roof, things also improved. Although I still hated her rules, Mrs. Brennan served cheeseburgers three or four nights a week; a menu that made me quite happy. And the family loved Monopoly, something near to my heart, so we had marathon games that went late into the evening and continued the next night from Baltic Avenue to Park Place and everywhere in between. Without school the next day, the Brennan's grew lax about bedtime and my stay there began to feel more like an extended sleepover than the juvenile detention center I had first detected. Before I knew it, the whole thing was over.

When my mom and dad returned from Europe to pick me up, I was thrilled to see them, but a piece of me was sad to leave my surrogate family. We had come so far in our ability to understand each other and I had clearly benefited by learning I had the wherewithal to adapt to alternative surroundings without the protective shield of my parents. As I drove home with them, full of the confidence that came with my newfound success, I asked the most important question I could think of: "Have you guys ever considered hanging your paper towels to dry?"

16
Beauty

The Haircut

It was a day like any other in my life. I rode the bus home from school and let myself in through the side door. I was alone but I knew my mother would be back from work soon so I opened a package of Twinkies, turned on the TV and waited for her at the kitchen table. It was my first year as a latchkey kid and, at nine-years old, I still breathed a sigh of relief every time I heard her car enter the driveway. A few months earlier, she had started teaching full-time at a school only fifteen minutes away but, due to our overlapping schedules, there was a half hour gap where I had to be brave and fly solo. As luck would have it, our house was located down a long gravel lane far away from any neighbors; an isolated spot perfectly designed to provoke anxiety.

There was a children's show called Zoom that ran from 3:30 to 4:00 p.m. and served as the perfect distraction until my mother's arrival each afternoon. Once it ended, without fail, I looked out our family room's front window for a sign of her; an act invariably rewarded within a few minutes in my past experience. But on this particular day, she didn't arrive when I expected. And as the minutes passed, a growing uneasiness overtook me. There was no way to reach her and I hesitated to call my father; knowing there was little he could do from his office in the city. With no other options, I decided to tough it out; trying every way possible to keep my thoughts occupied on something other than my mother's whereabouts.

At 4:30 p.m., I began to actively worry. Why is she late? I wondered. It was a winter day and I contemplated the possibility of an accident. It was starting to get dark and I imagined her hitting a patch of ice and going off the road into a ditch. By 5:00 p.m., my mind was getting the best of me as I pondered the possibility of a motherless future and checked the pantry for canned goods to eat if necessary. "Where is she?" I repeated aloud like a nervous tic.

Mercifully, relief arrived the moment I saw headlights coming up our drive. Meeting my mother in the mudroom as she entered the house, I couldn't contain myself.

"Mom, where were you?" I demanded in a tone I would otherwise never use.

"What do you mean?" she asked as she took off her coat and boots.

"I didn't know where you were," I said, my voice quivering.

"Love, I told you I was getting my hair cut after school."

"No you didn't, Mom. You didn't tell me."

"Are you sure?"

"Yes," I said emphatically.

She paused to observe my agitated condition.

"Oh, dear," she said. "I'm so sorry. I thought I told you but maybe I just told your sister."

My mother was always quick to believe my version of events and even quicker to apologize; two qualities I loved about her. She pulled me close and hugged me, acknowledging my upset and erasing it simultaneously.

"Will you play a game with me?" I asked, moving swiftly to secure additional attention.

"Of course," she said. "Let me use the bathroom and then I'll be right there."

For the next hour, I noticed nothing unusual about my mother's behavior. She played Aggravation with me on the floor of our family room with the same enthusiasm she always exhibited. She asked me about my day at school, offered to make me a snack and apologized several more times for making me fret. My mother made me feel better plain and simple; something I'd come to count on.

When my father returned from work, entering the house with a loud "hell-o," my mother excused herself from our game to go and greet him. This was not abnormal, but as I listened from the next room for the affectionate exchange I expected, something rare occurred. My mother exploded in sobs. "Oh, honey," she said, dissolving completely.

"What's wrong?" my father asked.

I froze; uncertain of what would come next. Had I done something wrong? Was I in trouble? The answer to both questions was no. Of all things, my mother was upset about her haircut. She thought it was too short.

I was completely puzzled. How could something so small cause her such upset? Hair grew back. Even I knew that. Plus my mother was not a vain woman. The fact she called it a "haircut" spoke volumes about her unaffected manner. Never once had I heard the words "manicure" or "pedicure" cross her lips. So it all didn't make sense. But what baffled me even more was why my mother hadn't told me she was so unhappy about her haircut. In my view, I was more than capable of empathy and would have liked the opportunity to return the favor bestowed on me earlier. All modesty aside, I had a very respectable record of feeling sorry for others and trying to comfort them. My friend, Davey Burdick, probably wouldn't have made it through the death of his goldfish without me.

Still, as I listened to my father soothe my mother's distress with words of support, I came to some sudden and stark realizations. By turning to my dad, my mother didn't intend to slight me; but rather to spare me from having to play the role of consoler. She didn't consider it a child's responsibility to be the person a parent turned to at such moments. Just as I looked to her for sympathy about things both big and small, she looked to my father. And as I thought about it more, it dawned on me that neither of my parents ever put me in the position of bearing the weight of their worries.

I concluded that this was as it should be and felt grateful for my parents' protective instincts. For the first time, I began to think about the meaning of marriage. I wasn't mature enough to place any value judgments on it, other than to understand that things would be very different for me if one of them wasn't around. In the end, I was left with only the question of why my mother cared about her hair so much; a mystery about which I can speculate now.

As a child, I never gave any thought to how my mother wore her hair. But as a young married woman up until the time she started teaching, my mother wore it long; putting it up in a beehive on special occasions. Looking at old pictures, it's easy to see how pretty and feminine it made her look. Her decision to cut it short was no doubt a practical one; made due to the realities of getting ready in the morning for work and getting children out the door for school. It made life easier when she had to be in her classroom by 7:00 a.m. each day.

Pragmatism, however, comes with a psychic cost. And with her newly cropped hair, I suspect my mother, despite her lack of vanity, felt the ebbing of something very real: perhaps her femininity, her youth or her time as a stay at home mom. Worse yet, with the bloom off the rose of marriage and the hard work of raising a family upon her, I have little doubt that, given my mother's sincere and dutiful nature, she felt a certain responsibility to remain attractive to my father. Not because he placed any expectation on her to do so, but rather from her own innate desire to please the person she loved most in the world.

Some people will say that's ridiculous and that my mother should have never concerned herself with anyone's approval but her own. My experience tells me those people are wrong. We all seek the approval of those close to us, and there's a beauty in doing things to make others happy; whether it's for a friend, a child or a spouse. Of course, it never really mattered whether my mother wore her hair long or short, up or down, in a beehive or a bob. Being beautiful was something that came naturally to her; something scissors could never touch.

17
Honesty

Bobby Sob

Before we moved to the country in 1974, we lived in a typical suburban subdivision of starter homes with young children in nearly every house. Within the boundaries of our track, I was free to roam for hours at a time; returning occasionally for food, equipment and medical supplies before disappearing again until dinner. Every kid I knew operated under the same arrangement and soon I was part of a pack that traveled together.

Our leader was Bobby Sobczak, the oldest and biggest of the bunch, who everyone called Bobby Sob. Bobby Sob ran his gang with an iron fist and made no pretense to covering it with a velvet glove. He was a tough sort who liked to hit you in the chin with his yo-yo if you didn't do what he said. Fearful of taking a

Duncan to the face, I found myself marching to Bobby Sob's intimidating beat.

Late one summer afternoon, Bobby Sob led us to a pond in a still developing area close to our neighborhood. Already playing there was Jackie Brasser, a little girl who lived four doors down the street from me. Jackie was pushing a small baby carriage with a plastic doll inside and she looked happily lost in her own world as we approached. Although she wasn't bothering us at all, Bobby Sob targeted her for harassment and instructed us to surround her. In a scene reminiscent of Lord of the Flies, we proceeded to encircle her and Bobby Sob began threatening to take the carriage away. I knew I should've stopped him, but I remained silent as the taunting continued and Jackie began to cry.

"Don't!" she shrieked, as Bobby Sob repeatedly reached in and pulled back empty-handed.

Eventually, he did it; grabbing the stroller away from her and tossing it into the pond. Jackie broke down and ran away, no doubt headed for home. Immediately afterward, despite her absence, Bobby Sob instructed us to lift a large log that was resting a few feet away and throw it on top of the carriage in order to fully sink it. Too weak to say no, I helped complete the dirty work as fast as I could, but the water was shallow and, instead of submerging the carriage, the log simply rested upon it leaving the wreckage for all to see. I felt sick. It was a terrible thing to do.

"If any of you say a word about this to anyone, I'll beat you to a pulp," Bobby Sob warned us as we disbanded for the evening.

Returning home, I skulked into the house and tried

How to Raise a Good Kid

to forget about the day's events. News of my activities, however, had already reached my mother.

"Mrs. Brasser just called me," my mom said; sending me into a tailspin.

"She did?"

"Yes. Did you throw Jackie's stroller into the pond?"

"No. I didn't throw it."

"Who did?"

I paused.

"I asked you a question," my mother said; determined to get an answer.

"I can't tell you," I said. "It might cost me my life."

"Was it Bobby Sob?"

I stared at my feet.

"Look at me," my mother said. "Was it Bobby Sob?"

Looking up, I nodded.

"Mrs. Brasser said there was a log on top of it in the water. Did you have anything to do with that?"

I nodded again as my eyes grew watery.

"I am extremely disappointed in you. And first thing tomorrow morning, you will be marching over to the Brasser's and apologizing for what you did. Do you understand me?"

With my father out of town, my mother gamely stepped into the role of disciplinarian. Although I'd been caught, it felt good to tell the truth; up until the moment I realized I'd ratted out Bobby Sob. If he found out, I'd face more than a yo-yo being flung at my chin. Death would stalk my every waking moment.

The next morning, I awoke hoping my mother had forgotten all about Jackie Brasser, but she hadn't. Sure enough, as soon as I finished eating my Captain Crunch and got dressed, I was pushed out the front door and commanded to make my pilgrimage.

"What if Bobby Sob sees me?" I asked, gripping my mother's hand tightly.

"Don't worry about Bobby Sob. He won't touch you."

Easy for you to say, I thought. You don't have to ride the bus with him.

Walking toward the Brasser's house, each of my steps more tentative than the last, I couldn't understand how I'd gotten myself into this predicament. Looking back, it's easy to see why I felt so overwhelmed. I was only five years old and my life had turned into a scene from a Hitchcock film.

Inching closer to my destination while nervously watching for any sign of Bobby Sob or his yo-yo, I finally saw the Brasser's front door. This was it. I was going to apologize and restore my honor and the honor of my family. I knew it was the right thing to do and nothing was going to stop me. End of story. Well . . . not quite.

Somehow, in the last ten feet before I reached the concrete stoop in front of the Brasser's house, I lost my nerve. And instead of ringing the bell, I ducked behind the large evergreen bush to the left of their door and hid. It was a shameful act motivated by forces I struggled to comprehend. Why was I afraid of saying I was sorry? Sure, it was hard to do. It was uncomfortable. It was embarrassing. But it was the right thing. So why couldn't I do it?

Still unable to figure it out after ten minutes behind the bush, I decided to go home.

"Did you apologize?" my mother asked as I entered the kitchen.

"Yes," I said; almost convincing myself that I had by simply going over there.

"I'm proud of you," she said.

I felt awful.

The following winter, with the baby carriage incident all but forgotten, I found myself building a snow fort with my sister, Pam, and a half dozen other kids in our back yard. The drifts were eight feet high and perfect for packing; and we used a set of hollow plastic boxes, shaped like rectangles to create icy white construction blocks. Nearing completion of the fort, our door was suddenly darkened by the arrival of Bobby Sob, who we hadn't seen lately. According to my mother, Bobby Sob's parents had enrolled him in a special school for children with behavioral problems but, whatever the case, he was back.

"Nice fort," he said derisively.

"It is a nice fort," my sister said; proud of the work we'd done.

"What if I knock it down?" Bobby Sob threatened.

"Don't you dare," my sister said.

Apparently Bobby Sob hadn't learned much at his special school because my sister's words did nothing to stop him from advancing toward her in a menacing fashion and picking up a shovel with the clear intention of using it to destroy our fort. Stepping into his pathway, my sister attempted to block Bobby Sob but he pushed her to the ground before swinging the shovel and blasting a large hole in the side of the structure.

This time, when faced with Bobby Sob's bullying, I wasn't weak. Something about the sight of him pushing my sister sent me into a rage; a fit of anger that welled up from a place I didn't know existed. Taking my own shovel, I ran up behind Bobby Sob and clubbed him in the head, drawing blood from his cheek and causing him to burst into tears — something I'd never seen.

"Why'd you do that?" he cried, grabbing his face with a gloved hand as blood dripped down on the snow.

Expecting him to charge me, I was shocked when he turned and left. I had successfully repelled him and I felt triumphant. All the bottled up emotions I'd been holding in about Bobby Sob were finally let out and it felt wonderful. Nevertheless, my sister and I agreed this wasn't something that needed to be shared at home and we kept our mouths shut when we went inside for cocoa.

Later that night, however, the telephone rang.

"Mrs. O'Dwyer, this is Marianne Sobczak — Bobby's mother. I'd like to speak with you about your son."

"Yes," my mother said. As she tells it, she was expecting a compliment.

"He is an animal!" Mrs. Sobczak declared, before explaining in detail how I'd conked Bobby in the head.

After the call, my mother, who was clearly upset, sat me down and asked me what happened. I described my efforts to defend Pam and, in doing so, I found myself recounting everything about my relationship with Bobby Sob. Finally, I confessed that I'd never apologized to Jackie Brasser for what I'd done to her baby carriage; an admission I had not planned to make. It just sort of came out and, once it did, I immediately saw the impact on my mother's face. She looked stunned and then distraught. But keeping her composure, she patiently explained that of all the things I'd done related to Bobby Sob, nothing was worse than lying to her.

The next day, she took me over to the Brasser's to apologize, assuring me I would feel better once I did. She was right and I figured our next stop would be the

Sobczak's to do the same, but we didn't go there. Instead, she took me sledding and we spent the afternoon having fun together. In her own way, my mother had imparted on me what she believed; stick up for your family, always tell the truth and stand up to bullies — three things I've never forgotten.

18
Patriotism

Once in a Lifetime

"Well, gang, I've done it this time. I've really done it."

Whenever my father said these words to our family, we all braced for impact; no one more so than my mother. Given her husband's history of seizing the moment, regardless of whether the moment was worth seizing, she was accustomed to finding out about things she would have to do long after it was possible to get out of doing them.

"What did you do?" she asked apprehensively.

"I ordered tickets for the Olympics."

"Way to go, Dad," I said, confident this idea was one of his good ones.

"What Olympics?" my mother asked.

"The Winter ones. In Lake Placid. In February," he

responded, his last word hanging in the air like an icicle.

"Will we be outdoors?" she asked with barely contained dread.

"A little bit," he said.

"Won't it be freezing?" my mother asked; her fear of the cold surfacing.

"Not at all. It's actually warmer up in the mountains."

"Honey, you know I've got terrible circulation and I hate to be cold," she reminded him.

"They'll have all kinds of heating stations. There's nothing to worry about. Plus, most of the events, like hockey and figure skating, are inside."

"I really don't want the kids to miss school," my mother said; trying another avenue to defeat the plan.

"They won't; not more than a week."

"A week? That's too long," she pleaded.

"Come on. It's the Olympics," my father said, immediately breaking into a forlorn rendition of the event's theme song. "Bommmm . . . bommmm . . . ba dumm dumm dumm . . ."

"I'm serious," my mother replied, cutting him off mid-theme.

"I promise they won't miss more than a day or two. This is a once in a lifetime opportunity for our family."

This was one of my father's favorite lines; one he used shamelessly to weaken his opposition on any number of matters, but somehow it worked. And just like that, with my mother out of ammunition, it was settled: we were headed for the 1980 Winter Olympics.

From that point forward, we mostly forgot about it. It was the summer of 1979 and with February still far off, we quickly gravitated back to the ordinary events of the

How to Raise a Good Kid 121

season; swimming, tennis and going for ice cream. Soon, the first day of school beckoned; keeping our attention miles away from Lake Placid, a condition that would have persisted if not for the events of November 4th when a group of Islamic students forcibly seized control of the American embassy in Iran and took 53 hostages.

Up until that point in my life, I had been blissfully unaware of conflict in the Middle East, radical terrorists and, frankly, geopolitical unrest of any sort; preferring to focus instead on important domestic issues, like determining the release date for the next Styx album. But the Iranian hostage crisis, as it was called by the media, forced me to leave my childlike views behind and realize that certain events occurring far away could affect me at home. Night after night we watched the news coverage on TV, and it wasn't long before reporters began asking what it meant for the Olympics. Seeing that I would soon be part of an international story, I suddenly had newfound respect for my father and his "once in a lifetime" promises.

As the winter months went on and the hostages remained under siege, tension grew and speculation ran rampant about what to expect in Lake Placid. Because an Iranian bobsled team or delegation of any sort was never a possibility given the nation's desert location, the question was whether any countries would take Iran's side and boycott the Olympics to show solidarity. I didn't understand at first how a sporting competition could be so politically-charged, but then I learned about the 1972 Munich games, where eleven Israeli athletes and coaches had been killed by terrorists, and the 1976 Montreal games, where 28 African countries boycotted due to a New Zealand rugby team's decision earlier that year to tour South Africa, despite its policy of apartheid. Whoa, I thought. Dad's really taking us into the heart of darkness.

By the time February arrived, American nationalism was at a fever pitch and all eyes turned to Lake Placid, where U.S. citizens would have a perfect opportunity to show their patriotism to the rest of the world. Ready to do my part, I climbed into the family car with proud determination; keenly aware that I was headed for the middle of a major happening and needed to support my homeland. Of course, it was 2:00 a.m. and I promptly fell asleep within ten minutes. In all the excitement of securing tickets to the games, my father neglected to book a hotel room (all of which were sold out by now). This meant an all-night drive to the Adirondacks, New York's largest mountain range, something I'm not sure my mother was pleased about. Nothing, however, could dampen my father's enthusiasm.

"The O'Dwyer family is going for the gold," he exclaimed as we pulled out of our driveway in the middle of a snowstorm.

"Do you think it's okay to go in this weather?" my mother asked, gripping her door handle and double-checking her seatbelt. "They're talking about closing the thruway," she said.

"It's absolutely fine," my father said, having never met a weather event that kept him from traveling. "Besides, if we don't go now, we won't make it on time."

"Why didn't we drive up yesterday and stay at a hotel?" my sister asked.

"Just go to sleep, all right," he replied, a bit perturbed.

How to Raise a Good Kid 123

When I woke up, we were in a parking lot surrounded by hundreds of other cars.

"Let's go," my father barked.

"Where are we going?" I asked.

"We have to get in line for the shuttle bus," my mother explained while handing us mittens, hats and scarves.

"That's right. The shuttle bus is going to take us to our events," my father said.

"Which events do we have tickets for, Dad?" I asked. "We've got ice hockey tickets, right?"

"Well, not exactly," he said.

"We don't?" I asked, unable to hide my disappointment.

"Do have figure skating tickets, Dad?" my sister asked.

"Not quite," he said. "Look, guys, the tickets I got were handed out by lottery so I didn't get to pick the sports. It was all luck of the draw."

"So what did we draw?" my mother asked. "The opening ceremonies?"

"No," my father said.

"Speed skating?" my sister asked.

"No, not that either," he said.

"Then what did we draw, Dad?" I asked excitedly.

Like a man tasked with selling steak to a group of vegetarians, my father gave us his best pitch.

"We drew the second run of the men's giant slalom and the 90 meter ski jump. How does that hit you?"

For ten seconds, it was dead quiet inside the car.

"Are those held indoors?" my mother asked, breaking the silence.

"Not really," my father said.

With one collective groan, we climbed out of our

station wagon and stepped into the Arctic Circle. Although it was sunny, a strong current of frigid air whipped us as we trekked toward a distant mass of people waiting for shuttle buses to the various venues.

Despite the weather, the crowd we joined fifteen minutes later was bursting with jingoistic fervor; chanting "U-S-A" repeatedly and staring hard at anyone speaking a foreign language. Taking our place among the throng, we added our voices to the chorus with gusto and, for a brief moment in time, we believed that maybe, just maybe, my father's decision to drag us outside in life-threatening temperatures to support our country's athletes was not completely insane.

"U-S-A! U-S-A! U-S-A!" we bellowed, standing next to a man whose winter hat had a picture of Mickey Mouse saying, "Hey, Iran," and doing something with his middle finger I'd never seen Mickey do. Through the bright, white glare of sunshine bouncing off snow, we saw my father's vision for an unforgettable O'Dwyer family outing.

Two hours later, however, that vision was getting cloudy. Underestimating the number of attendees, the Olympic organizers failed to send enough shuttle buses; leaving the horde of hundreds outside for far longer than recommended given the sub-zero conditions.

"Mom, my feet are freezing," I said.

"Mine, too, Mom," my sister echoed.

"I know kids. Honey, did you put the wool liners I gave you into the kids' boots?" my mother asked my father.

"What liners?" he asked.

And so it went as we got colder, the mob grew uglier and bus sightings remained rare. Eventually, chants of

"U-S-A" gave way to something a bit more practical.

"Where's the effin bus? Where's the effin bus?" they shouted over and over.

"What's 'effin' mean, Mom?" I asked.

After three hours of standing, we made it onto a shuttle bus, stumbling to the back and huddling like immigrants rescued from icy waters. My father, however, was not ready to give up on his Olympic dream.

"The good news is we're still going to make the 90 meter ski jump. It only started an hour ago," he said.

"You mean we have to go back outdoors?" my mother asked, her frozen hands fumbling to undo the emergency Thermos of hot coffee she'd packed.

"I can't feel my toes, Dad," I said.

"Come on, guys," my father said. "This is a once in lifetime experience."

"Let's hope so," my mother said, shivering as she tried to affix her lips to the Thermos.

Higher and higher into the mountains we climbed until, mercilessly, the bus driver stopped and told us we'd reached our destination; casting us back out into Antarctica.

Hiking northward like an ill-fated Everest expedition, we soon stood somewhere on the side of Whiteface Mountain watching colored dots in the distance launch themselves high into the air off an enormous ski jump. But after two Finns, a Brit and a Jamaican completed their runs, our spectating came to an abrupt end. Fearing one of us might suffer the loss of an appendage if we stayed any longer; my mother led my sister and me to the nearest Red Cross station for medical attention while my father reluctantly followed behind.

"The American skier hasn't even gone yet," he called after

her; hoping he might earn a temporary stay of the decision.

"I don't care," my mother called back. "The kids are popsicles."

The rest of our Olympic experience was spent staring at the ceiling of a tent as a team of EMTs and paramedics tried to bring our toes back to life. Driving home later that day, I think my father felt defeated. He desperately wanted his family to have a memorable time but nothing had gone according to plan and now he wondered if it had all been worth the effort.

A few days later, like most Americans, we gathered around the TV and watched the U.S. hockey team defeat the U.S.S.R. juggernaut 4-3 in what now is the most famous Olympic hockey game of all-time. With the Cold War raging and our fellow citizens being held hostage in Iran, we banded together and rooted wildly for our country to win. And when the announcer, Al Michaels, asked, "Do you believe in miracles?" As the last seconds of the final period ticked away, the collective answer in our family room was a resounding, "yes."

Of course, you could argue that the game didn't change anything. It didn't improve our relations with Russia or free the hostages, and it wasn't even the squad's final test, which would occur two days later against Finland. But at our house, the U.S. hockey team's victory over the Soviets felt like a victory for us and that night, our family, like millions of other American families, got its gold medal. After much disappointment, we were lifted up unexpectedly and were grateful for it.

These days, when the topic of the 1980 U.S. Olympic hockey team comes up, I'm quick to point out that I was in Lake Placid that year. After which, I'm invariably asked: "Were you at the hockey game with the Russians?"

"Of course, I was," I always say, embellishing a bit. "My father got tickets and drove us there in the middle of the night through a snowstorm."

"What was it like?" They always want to know and so I answer.

"It's hard to describe," I say. "It was truly a once in a lifetime experience."

19
Punishment

The Green Chair

Punishment in my home as a child was black and white and green. Black and white in that the boundaries of acceptable behavior were clearly marked, and green in that the place you received your spankings when you traveled outside those boundaries was known as the green chair; a wide, high-backed seat with ugly olive fabric.

My parents had a traditional marriage with a division of labor that fell strictly along historical gender lines so law and order belonged to my dad. This was a natural fit given his military background and love of World War II prison break movies. Every evening when he came home from work, he would ask my mother for a report as to how my sister and I had behaved. If the report wasn't good, a fairly violent beating would soon follow. Unfortunately for us, the time out had not been invented yet.

The greatest offense one could commit in our house was to be fresh, my father's code word for speaking disrespectfully to either him or my mother. If you shot your mouth off at the dinner table or anywhere else in a way that displeased him, he would ask you if you were being fresh. Delivered in an angry tone that made it clear he had already made up his mind, this question was strictly rhetorical. Before you could offer up any kind of verbal defense, you were informed that he was frosted; a point driven home by the veins bulging from his forehead and neck. What invariably followed from my father's mouth were the six most frightening words in the English language: "Meet me at the green chair."

Being summoned to the green chair inspired complete and utter terror in me. I don't know exactly how it feels to be sent to the electric chair, but I share a kindred spirit with those currently sitting on death row. Of course, the trip to the family room and the anticipation of being struck were worse than the actual spanking. When I was sent to the green chair, my sister would often cry and I would do the same for her. It was always a shock to the system. One minute you're eating a grilled cheese sandwich or beef taco with your family and feeling pretty good about life; the next minute you're a contestant on Fear Factor.

As he explained to me in later years, my father had two components to his unified theory of punishment. The first was that parents had to follow through on threats. He refused to be the father who constantly threatened to pull the car over but never did; this was a sure way to lose your child's respect and turn him into a

How to Raise a Good Kid

juvenile delinquent or spree killer. The second part was that parents had to maintain a united front. If my father wasn't around and I made the error of being fresh or otherwise acting out, my mother would simply advise me that the matter would be resolved when my father got home. And no matter how much I begged her not to say anything, she refused to break ranks with my dad.

Once my father's car pulled up, I ignored my overwhelming desire to go hide in my bedroom and, instead, ran headlong into the hurricane. Meeting him at the front door with a cold bottle of beer swiped from the refrigerator, I would greet him like a General returning from battle. "How was your day, Dad? You look tired. Let me take your briefcase," I'd say in my cheeriest voice, throwing my arms around his waist. At that moment, he immediately knew I was pleading guilty and throwing myself on the mercy of the court.

Given the unlikelihood of a reprieve, I always prepared for my spankings, when possible, by dressing appropriately. This involved donning multiple pairs of underwear, at least two pairs of corduroys and a Hardy Boys mystery which I would strategically shove down the back of my pants; all to cushion the impending blows. After removing the book and putting me across his lap as he sat in the green chair, my father would administer perhaps a half dozen, rapid-fire whacks with his hand to my buttocks and then send me to my room to think things over. Shortly thereafter, with my eyes wet, my nose runny and my body still heaving, I would hear the door open and see my father enter. Sitting down next to me, he would try to comfort me, explain why what I'd done was unacceptable and bring me downstairs for dinner.

Despite the messy emotions, the process was fairly tidy.

Today, corporal punishment is a taboo subject. Studies documenting its deleterious effect on self-esteem sprout like kudzu and admitting you spank to others is like saying you still enjoy cigarettes, traditional marriage or voting Republican. But before anyone labels my father some kind of monster or gets hysterical and calls their local department of child and family services, let me add some context and perspective.

I was raised in the 1970's, long before the advent of the everybody gets a trophy and an iPad approach to parenting that now seeks to guard the egos of children from day-to-day setbacks at any cost. This was still the age of spare the rod and spoil the child, and my father was doing what his father had done and what he genuinely believed to be in our best interests. More and more people forget that, far from the now-disparaged mode of discipline, spanking was a respectable and normal part of parenting. In fact, not spanking was viewed as irresponsible by most.

One unintended consequence of my father's intense anger was that it taught me how to get mad in a way that frightened people. After demonstrating that ability to myself and others on a handful of occasions as a young man, however, I realized that my outbursts left me emotionally shaken and physically spent; alienating others while rarely accomplishing their intended objective. Acknowledging that this approach didn't work for me, I stopped using it; letting my capability for anger atrophy like a muscle I no longer used. I don't know what the lasting impact was on my sister. We only joke about the green chair; seemingly in agreement that any sober analysis would be pointless.

I harbor no ill will toward my dad for spanking me. To the contrary, I'm glad he did. I learned in a memorable way that my actions had consequences and that treating others with respect was important; lessons that have served me well in adulthood. Perhaps he could he have dialed down the intensity a bit. When he worked himself into a lather, like a wild animal whose foot was caught in a trap, it was truly frightening. But he set clear boundaries, enforced them consistently and combined structured discipline with lots of love and a bit of mayhem.

It may not have worked for every kid, but I think my father's approach to punishment gave me a measure of internal toughness that I continue to rely upon. These days, whenever I'm faced with a situation that promises to be hell on Earth, I remind myself that there's nothing they can throw at me that I can't handle. After all, I've already been to the green chair.

20
Faith

Rock, God and Santa Claus

At age eight, I had one all-consuming passion: rock and roll — a genre of music I understood to include KC and the Sunshine Band, Sonny and Cher, and anything else played on Casey Kasem's *American Top Forty* countdown. Listening to his program every Sunday morning was my religion. Unfortunately, my parents' religion was Presbyterianism which required going to church, a diversion that cut into prime Casey time, and a place where transistor radios with ear pieces were not only frowned upon but confiscated.

I feared this burgeoning conflict was stunting my spiritual growth. The way I saw it, every week, because of God, I missed the final hour of the countdown and remained unaware of the top ten songs in the nation. I knew in my heart this could not be God's plan; forcing me to wander the halls of elementary school like a social pariah armed only with the ability to recite songs forty through eleven. If the situation persisted, I would likely never marry or raise children.

Given the stakes, I patiently explained to my father one Sunday morning that this state of affairs was creating a wedge between me and the man upstairs, and that the only solution I saw was for me to stay home while the rest of the family attended services. Upon their return, I would give them a full run down of the top ten hits and, if they felt like briefly sharing the high points from Reverend Boak's sermon, I would certainly be glad to listen. This struck me as a fair bargain and one we could all live with on a going forward basis.

To my great disappointment, my father did not see things exactly the same way. To his credit, he didn't react like the pastor in Footloose and call rock and roll the devil's music (understandable considering the movie hadn't been made yet). But he did tell me to take the tie I had wrapped around my head and put it back around my neck before pointing me toward our waiting wood-paneled station wagon in the garage. The solution, he said, was for me to pray about the problem at church.

And so I did; asking Lord God to lead me out of my musical desert and into the promised land of the Ozark Mountain Daredevils, Captain and Tennille and Leo Sayer; all rock and roll giants in my book at the time. Christmas was fast approaching so I wrote Santa, just as a back-up, and asked him to bring me something to solve this crisis. After all, these were the days before e-mail and instant messaging and I knew it might take God

How to Raise a Good Kid

awhile to get back to me given his crazy busy schedule.

Meanwhile at school, as December lumbered onward, I buried myself in work — learning my state capitols and consciously steering conversations away from the dangerous topic of classic rock. When asked what I wanted for Christmas, I lied; rattling off platitudes about G. I. Joe and Super Toe and making sure not to mention music. For the first time, when adults spoke of holiday stress, I understood.

On Christmas Eve, I pulled my father aside for a serious fireside chat. I needed to know if God and Santa Claus had been in touch lately about my problem. He assured me they were close friends and that the odds were good they had discussed it. Tucked into bed, I drifted to sleep that night with cautious optimism and Winnie the Pooh, my consigliere.

The next morning, I was like a kid on Christmas (my NFL footy pajamas and trusty blanket were dead giveaways). Ignoring all etiquette, I tore open each of my gifts like a 401(k) statement from 1999. By the end, I had received some lovely items, including a Nerf football, but nothing in my pile was going to get me out of going to church every week. And if I had to go to church, I couldn't listen to the end of Casey Kasem's countdown and learn the top ten songs in the nation. Staring into the endless void underneath the Christmas tree, I knew my life would never be the same. If God and Santa Claus couldn't help me; nobody could.

Determined to maintain my composure, I put on my bravest face; refusing to wallow in self-pity like some kind of spoiled ingrate. Nevertheless, my father picked up on my high level of distress. Perhaps it was my hysterical crying and accompanying hyperventilation but, looking back now, it's really anybody's guess how he did it. Calmly, he looked over to me.

"I think I saw one more box behind the tree with your name on it."

"Really?" I asked, wiping the snot from my nose on the sleeve of my pajamas.

He began digging down below the Douglas-fir in our family room. Seconds later, from the nether regions of the mighty tree, he brought out a small package unlike any other I'd seen that morning. It was beat up and bedraggled; like it had traveled a long way, and it was wrapped in crinkled brown paper with a small tag that had my name on it.

"Open her up," my father said.

What happened next can only be described as a rock-n-roll miracle. Inside the box was a brand new, shiny, state-of-the-art Panasonic tape recorder; an invention so great it made Wacky Packages and penicillin look pedestrian.

"You can tape songs from the radio," my father said.

I was ecstatic and had I been told that we as a people would never surpass this engineering achievement — this unrivaled feat of science — I would have believed it. It was everything one could hope for and more.

From that day forward, I never missed the end of Casey's countdown; taping the last hour and returning to the results after church like an archeologist on a dig. I'll never know whether it was God or Santa Claus who came to my rescue but I want to thank them publicly for saving my childhood. As for my father, I want to thank him for his keen eyesight. Who knows what would have happened if he hadn't spied that package behind the tree.

21
Resiliency

Winthrop I Hardly Knew Thee

One day in fourth grade, my music teacher, Mrs. Bantam, asked me to stay after class. This was never good news so I braced myself when I heard her stomach-churning request and watched helplessly as the other kids escaped into the hallway.

"How would you like to be in the high school musical?" she asked once everyone had left.

Although I played my recorder competently, I wasn't sure what I'd done to catch Mrs. Bantam's eye.

"Me in the high musical?" I asked.

At nine years of age, my theatre experience consisted of a small walk-on role in the third grade production of Don't Fire 'til You See the Whites of Their Eyes, a revolutionary war drama in which I played the back end of George Washington's horse. My time toiling in obscurity, however, was about to end. The high school was staging The Music Man and they needed a little boy for the prominently featured role of Winthrop; kid brother of Marian the librarian, the love interest of band leader Harold Hill.

"You've got star quality," Mrs. Bantam told me.

"I do?"

She nodded and that was it. I was going to be a stage and screen icon. Her words went straight to my head. Forget Plan B.

Winthrop's role required that I sing a solo of the song Gary, Indiana and my father, an amateur piano player, assured me he knew it; no sheet music required. With only one week until my try-out, we began a nightly ritual of rehearsals followed by hot tea with lemon at my mother's insistence. Like a deluded American Idol contestant, I convinced myself, with the aid of others, that I was pretty good, chirping my happy version of the song with full encouragement from my parents.

"How do I sound?" I asked, my voice cracking like an egg on every third note.

"Like a star. You heard Mrs. Bantam," my father replied.

Back at school, I learned that my primary competition for the role of Winthrop was my classmate Jimmy Woodarski. Jimmy was a nice kid, but he had wispy, unkempt blond hair and a lisp, and he wore an enormous back brace due to his curved spine. Poor Jimmy, I thought. They're only giving him a chance because they feel sorry for him and he doesn't even know it. Music Man was a period piece and there was no place in 1950's Iowa for a kid with a massive hunk of steel strapped to his back.

Try-outs arrived and my father drove me to the high school; our collective confidence brimming. Gar-y Indiana, Gar-y Indiana, Gar-y Indiana. Let me say it once again," I sang loudly as we sped closer to my destiny.

"How do I sound?" I asked.

"Like a Broadway legend," my father answered. "This try-out is a mere formality."

Jimmy went first and, wouldn't you know it, the kid wasn't half bad. His version sounded a bit different than mine but, warbling away, he followed the piano player's cues and acquitted himself in a very respectable manner. To my dismay, Mr. Denison, the director, was a bit more enthusiastic about Jimmy's performance than I would have liked.

"Great job, Jimmy. I love the lisp," he said, as if Jimmy had any choice in the matter. "It's just like Winthrop's. You must've watched the movie," Mr. Denison gushed.

I pulled my father aside.

"Dad, there's a movie we could've watched?" I asked.

"Well, yes, but I didn't think it was necessary," he said. "Not with your talent," he added.

"Winthrop has a lisp?" I asked.

"If I recall, he may have been a bit lispy," my father said.

My confidence in tatters, I climbed the stairs leading to the stage convinced that Jimmy was Winthrop. All I had left to comfort me was Jimmy's back brace which thankfully he was still wearing.

Up on the boards, the first thing I noticed was the size of the stage. It was cavernous and the piano player, located below in the orchestra pit, looked very far away.

"Are you ready?" Mr. Denison asked.

I took a deep breath and nodded. Star quality, do

your thing, I thought as the pianist began playing the introduction to Gary, Indiana. Bursting into song, I immediately sensed that I was out of sync with the music and stopped singing.

"Can we start again?" I asked.

Mildly perturbed, Mr. Denison signaled the pianist to start again. This time, I quickly realized I was not only out of sync with the music but also many of the lyrics. My father taught the song to me from memory and evidently a few details concerning its pacing and themes had escaped him.

"For crying out loud, what's the problem here?" Mr. Denison barked.

"Dad?" I asked meekly in the direction of my father, who was now attempting to slouch down in his seat as far as humanly possible.

"We practiced it differently at home," my father said, standing up and walking to the piano. "Let me try it with him."

"Fine, but you've got to use the sheet music," Mr. Denison ordered.

"It's on the stand," the pianist said.

It was then I learned my father and I had an identical level of experience when it came to reading music — none. He tried his best, launching into something vaguely resembling what was written down but, given the traumatic events of the prior five minutes, neither of us was able to pull off the miracle required.

"I don't think this is going to work out," Mr. Denison said, his voice absent of empathy as he dispatched us.

Dissolving into tears, I left the auditorium humiliated. As I sniffled and snorfed on the ride home, my father kept apologizing to me again and again until I began to feel a bit sorry for him.

"Don't worry, Dad," I said. "It's not your fault. I found out that Jimmy had a professional vocal coach."

"Really?" my dad asked.

"Yes," I continued. "Turns out he was a ringer. We never stood a chance," I said.

"Figures," my dad replied.

"How do you think Mom will take the bad news?" I asked.

"She'll be fine as long as you are," he said.

Finally, we reached home and pulled into our garage.

"Dad, do you think I have star quality?" I asked, looking him straight in the eyes after he turned off the ignition.

"In spades, son," he said. "In spades."

22
The Wisdom of Mothers

Long Before eBay

Years from now, when archeologists dig in my parents' attic, they will unearth the strangest collection of artifacts they've ever encountered. Long before rare and valuable or odd and unwanted items could be sold through online auctions, kids collected things for reasons nobody understood. Growing up, I was one of those kids.

Like everyone I knew, I collected cards. Baseball, football, hockey, basketball, Star Wars, Close Encounters of the Third Kind, Planet of the Apes, Six Million Dollar Man; the list was endless. I also collected stickers, especially Wacky Packages which depicted everyday products in a light less favorable. In Wacky world, among other mutations, Crest toothpaste became Creep, Wonder Bread turned into Blunder Bread and Captain

Crunch was Captain Crud; each metamorphosis appealing perfectly to my subversive and juvenile comic sensibilities at the time.

I kept all my cards and stickers in a stack of Adidas shoe boxes bound with rubber bands and spent countless happy hours trading them with my fellow collectors. Some I held dear and some I put in the spokes of my banana-seat bike, but I wasn't satisfied collecting cards and stickers only, and I began to look for expansion opportunities.

My parents, no doubt thrilled I was interested in something other than watching TV, obliged; introducing me to stamp and coin collecting. In a blink, I had notebooks packed with postage from distant places like Ethiopia and Bolivia displayed in plastic sleeves, and velvet-lined cases full of U.S. pennies, among others, from as far back as 1906. With visions of their son as a world-class philatelist or numismatist in their eyes, my mother and father repeatedly took me to the local mall to indulge my acquisitive eye. Yet, it wasn't enough.

Unexplainably, I also started to collect TV Guide and Sports Illustrated magazines. Week after week, I added to the growing stack in my room, drawing a few questions but never condemnation from my mother, who simply cleaned around them and double-checked the batteries in the fire detectors.

As the resident saint of our family, my mother and her laissez-faire attitude would soon be tested by what came next. Having recently discovered a taste for Dannon yogurt, I decided to collect the protective plastic lids that came with each cup. I also determined that empty Tic Tac containers would be valuable in the future and that stockpiling them now was a wise and prudent move.

To no one's surprise, within weeks of these developments, my bedroom began to resemble a neighborhood yard sale. Overflowing boxes of yogurt lids and Tic Tac containers, which I'd begun to horde, fought for floor space with towering magazine stacks and shoeboxes. And to make matters worse, I had lost control of my stamp and coin collections; failing to keep them organized, so loose Peruvian postage and Canadian currency were littered about adding to the disorder.

Still, my excesses were not curbed. Shortly thereafter, I embarked on a new mission: collecting autographs. Quickly discovering that there were few A-list stars living in Rochester, New York, I became less discriminating and went the B-list route; pursuing signatures from local luminaries such as Murph the Surf, who owned Murphy's, my favorite pizza place, and my sister, who I was confident would go on to do great things. For me, starting collections had become an addiction with no end in sight.

Then one day, not long after school let out for the summer, my friend, Tommy Indovino, invited me to his older cousin's house to see something he said would change my life.

"What is it?" I asked. "Is he going to blow something up with an M-80?"

When it came to firecrackers, the M-80 was the ultimate and could destroy your average mailbox in a single explosion.

"Better," Tommy said.

"Is it a tree fort?"

"Better," Tommy said.

"Does he have a mini-bike?" I asked.

"You'll have to wait and see."

Once we arrived, Tommy's cousin, Anthony, led

us down to his basement; a brown-carpeted labyrinth of lava lamps, Rush posters and beaded gateways. In a back room, partitioned off with faux-wood paneling, we traveled past an air hockey table until we came upon a sight so magnificent I dropped the packet of Pop Rocks I was eating.

"Whoa. That's incredible," I said.

"It's the biggest collection in the world," Anthony said.

"Really?" I asked.

"Well, I'm pretty sure," Anthony said, his confidence dipping briefly. "I've never seen a bigger one. Have you?"

"No. Absolutely not," I said. "It's amazing."

With fluorescent light glistening off every can, the beer can pyramid in front of me took up an entire wall.

"How many cans do you have?" I asked.

"459. And you better not steal any," Anthony said.

"Oh, I wouldn't steal any, I swear."

"Better not or I'll pound you," Anthony said.

"He's not lying," Tommy added. "He will pound you."

"Where did you get the cans?" I asked, hoping to divert the conversation away from my violent demise.

"Mostly at the town dump in Perinton," Anthony said. "They've got all kinds of good stuff there."

The next day, there was only one place I wanted to go. I got on my bike and rode to Perinton, one town over, and happily found a largely unattended gold mine of garbage. I briefly considered starting my own beer can collection but I knew that wouldn't go over well at home so I shifted my focus slightly and began to fill a Hefty plastic bag I'd brought with every different soda can I could find.

Picking through the trash, I was in nirvana. I never

How to Raise a Good Kid

realized how many companies made soda or how many different flavors there were to drink. Filling up my bag for an hour with familiar brands like Fanta, Shasta, 7-Up, Coke, Tab, Canada Dry and Pepsi, as well as others I'd never heard of, I left the dump like Santa Claus with a large sack over my shoulder and a smile on my face.

"What in the bag?" my mother asked nervously as I traipsed into the kitchen.

"Soda cans," I said. "I'm starting a collection."

"Another one?" she asked, letting her concern show for a split second.

My mother is a neat and orderly person to the extreme and I knew the increasingly cluttered state of our house was starting to threaten her sanity.

"I'll keep them in the basement, Mom."

"Where did you get them?"

"Perinton," I said, purposefully leaving out a few crucial details.

"Where in Perinton?"

"The town dump," I said, fully expecting my mother to banish me and my cans to the garage immediately.

Strangely, she did no such thing.

"All right," she said. "But you've got to wash them out first. You can do it here in the sink."

"Okay," I replied, bringing my sack to the center of the kitchen and opening it.

As I pulled the first empty can out of the bag and went to put it in the sink, something unexpected occurred. A large bee crawled out from inside; startling me in the process.

"Yikes!" I said, dropping it in the basin and watching the bee fly off for parts unknown.

"What is it?" my mother asked.

"There was a bee in the can," I said.

Looking around, I began to see bees everywhere. By opening the bag, I had let out a large group of angry insects who'd been residing inside my new prize possessions.

"Quick. Get the Raid and my fly swatter from under the sink," my mother said.

Doing as told, I was impressed by my mother's state of calm amidst chaos as I haphazardly sprayed Raid in all directions and she took repeated swings at our tormentors, who were clearly mad about being evicted from their homes. The bees were everywhere, menacing us in the small space of our kitchen and putting up quite a fight. Finally, we brought the situation under control and vanquished the last of the bugs, but not before one of them stung my mother's leg.

"Yeowch!" she cried, before getting a bag of ice to reduce the swelling.

Although my mother never complained or got angry at me, I felt rotten and the entire incident sapped my desire for soda cans and pyramids. Over time, my passion for collecting things waned and the innumerable objects I'd gathered were boxed or bagged and then moved to my parents' attic.

Years later, when I was grown and out of the house, I asked my mother if she'd kept all my memorabilia from the Tic Tac containers to the TV Guides. "Of course," she replied. "I couldn't bring myself to throw your collections out. They're a part of you."

And then I understood why my mother had so willingly endured it all; why she had put up with the cards and the cans, the stamps and the coins, the yogurt lids and the Tic Tac containers. She was determined to support me in all my endeavors no matter the personal inconvenience to her; refusing to squelch the enthusiasms of her son whatever the cost for one simple reason. She loved me and, by doing so, she taught me about the one thing of true value to collect in this world.

23
Love and Marriage

50 Years On

From time to time, when my parents took a trip, they left my sister and me with our grandparents. To get to Grandma and Granddad's place, we never went "over the river and through the woods" as the old song goes. We took the New York State Thruway; exiting somewhere around Schenectady and driving south to a speck of a town called Esperance. Bea and Red (as others called them) retired there after a life near New York City; buying some land and building a pretty, yellow ranch home on a hill with a long view of the valley below. It was a quiet, out-of-the-way spot that felt like Mars to me each time I landed. And though I complained there was nothing to do during these visits, I now see how lucky I was to be bored; a condition that allowed me to slow down and see things I'd never forget.

It's been thirty years, but my memories of their house are vivid. My grandmother had extensive gardens and, come summertime, her sunflowers craned toward our car to greet us as we pulled into the driveway. The yard was perfectly kept thanks to my grandfather, who seemingly spent half his time with a lawnmower and the other half with a rake. When the front door opened, I always smelled something funny: a faintly sweet and comforting scent from cigars, pipes and cigarettes; although admittedly I failed to recognize the source back then. It was just the way Grandma and Granddad smelled. Looking back, I'm sure I inhaled enough second hand smoke to bring a class-action lawsuit against them, but the other things I breathed in while visiting more than made up for any damage to my lungs. To my great benefit, I got to observe, up close and personal, the real life functioning of a lifelong marriage. This was no small thing and the lessons I learned by watching their well-oiled machine of matrimony were many.

For starters, it's absolutely critical to marry someone whose strengths complement your weaknesses. For instance, my grandmother was quite excitable. She could go from zero to DEFCON 1 in an instant if a crisis arose; such as the discovery of low levels of milk, fruit salad or flavored icy pops. My grandfather on the other hand was a calming presence who could diffuse such a situation by reminding my grandmother of the extra icy pops in the basement freezer or by insisting he wasn't in the mood for fruit salad that night. This kept her happy and prevented any number of aneurysms.

How to Raise a Good Kid 155

Another thing I came to truly understand was the importance of a solid transportation plan in a relationship. My grandmother couldn't drive or, more accurately, wouldn't drive after the "incident" in '64 which she steadfastly refused to discuss. My mom said it involved ice, snow and a department store Santa Claus, but the details were sketchy. Fortunately, my grandfather was licensed to operate a motor vehicle in the State of New York and enjoyed firing up his Nash Rambler and ferrying Grandma back and forth from Price Chopper, where she could stock up on frozen corn niblets, more icy pops and enough canned goods to survive a nuclear holocaust.

Couples, I concluded, must stick together in sickness and in health, but particularly in sickness. My grandmother had a lot of illnesses. By her own count, she'd had 23 major operations and she took a special pride in showing her grandchildren the damage that surgery and time had wrought. For me, this meant witnessing her mastectomy scar (on several separate occasions), her false teeth, and her psoriasis, among other things, and hearing in-depth tales of Scarlet Fever, arthritis, cataracts and loosened stool. By God's good graces, my grandfather knew the way to the hospital and possessed a special affection for waiting rooms where he could pretend to read magazines like Redbook and Ladies Home Journal. The fact that Grandma was battling three or four diseases at any given time and had a nightstand full of enough prescription medication to make Elvis blush never seemed to faze him. He just kept taking her to the doctor.

At the same time, although devotion and togetherness are wonderful, it's important not to lose yourself in a marriage. This means maintaining your own interests;

something my grandparents managed to do quite well. Adhering to the old adage about standing side by side like pillars supporting the same roof, they could go hours without talking to each other; my grandfather listening to Dixieland in the living room while my grandmother sat at the end of her bed watching a nine-inch black and white portable TV, pausing only for meals. My grandfather relished being left alone and, lucky for him, my grandmother respected and honored that wish. Of course, there were exceptions; like if there was a fly to kill in the bedroom or something big like that, in which case she'd holler for my grandfather like she was on fire. But for the most part, she only did that every 10 minutes or so and the rest of the time she left him in total peace.

Money can be an issue in a marriage so you have to agree on a mutually satisfactory fiscal path. My grandfather didn't believe in credit cards and, by coincidence, my grandmother didn't have any; so they were well-matched on this account. Cash and carry was their policy; one that turned my grandmother into a first-rate haggler. To my grandfather's great satisfaction, his wife could acquire her entire winter wardrobe in an afternoon at Two Guys with nothing but a twenty dollar bill and a coupon for kitty litter.

And speaking of wardrobes, it is a mistake to subject your spouse to any kind of extreme makeover; wasting money on things they'll never wear. Instead, you must develop an appreciation for your better half's unique sense of style; a rule my grandparents abided by assiduously. Although my grandmother's clothes were a campaign of shock and awe comprised of brightly-colored, loose-fitting, floral tablecloths with openings for her appendages, I never heard my grandfather heap anything on her but praise. Even copious amounts of costume jewelry in a shade completely unrelated to the rest of her outfit drew nothing but an approving smile. To him, she was beautiful.

Admiration aside, like any twosome, Bea and Red weren't always in perfect harmony. Some people think that when two people argue constantly their marriage must be an unhappy one. This is not so. My grandparents loved to bicker about pretty much anything and especially about the weather, what to eat for dinner, President Nixon and the televangelist my grandfather thought was channeling God. The biggest blow-ups, however, stemmed from my grandmother's status as America's most notorious backseat driver. At any given moment, she would hijack a perfectly pleasant drive by screaming, "Watch out, Red!" at 200 decibels. This would occur about 12 times during an average twenty minute trip until we finally made it home. For some reason, these outbursts always made my grandfather thirsty; for as soon as we pulled into the driveway, he would mutter, "I need a drink." For the most part, if any conversation in the car or elsewhere got too heated, my grandfather would take the high road by pronouncing my grandmother's position, "completely asinine," and then retreating to the garage to refinish a piece of furniture or build a dinette set; which brings me to another key point.

When tensions boil over in a relationship, it is helpful if each side has a place to escape to for awhile to regain their equilibrium and remember what it is they like about the other person. My grandfather went to the garage, but Grandma's domain was her kitchen, an all-tangerine affair where she was free to smoke Carltons, drink Sanka and ponder the next porcelain figurine to add to her Li'l Stinkers collection. If she'd had cross words with Granddad, she could be found at the circular pine table where we ate most meals rubbing her hands together, worrying aloud about the price of butter and debating whether or not she had enough ribbon candy in the event of a Soviet invasion. Eventually, they'd both cool down and normalcy would resume.

Through it all, what I saw was that marriage requires sacrifice and devotion more than anything. Whatever my grandmother's faults or eccentricities, nobody topped her in these two areas. A city kid from Brooklyn, she never shared my grandfather's dream of retiring to the country but she embraced it for him without complaint and set about the task of making their home as warm and welcoming as any. She cooked and cleaned and sewed and, on occasion, when she heard a jazz song emanating from the living room that she liked, such as Bill Bailey, she would saunter in and start dancing like a flapper girl with one hand in the air and the other pressed against her stomach; shimmying forward and back and singing with a huge smile on her face; telling my grandfather in her own way that she was happy with him and happy with her life. She did loads of laundry and dishes, wrote hundreds of Christmas cards and thank you notes, took thousands of car trips, and ran the household day after day, year after year; always by my grandfather's side.

In the summer of 1981, our entire family gathered at The Old Tavern, a restored inn in Grafton, Vermont, to celebrate my grandparents' 50th wedding anniversary. Having met at college in the 1920's, married in 1931, welcomed daughters in 1936 and 1940 and raised their family, they had done it all and this was to be their crowning moment. On a beautiful July evening, with the sun setting and everyone looking just so, we moved as a group to a converted barn on the inn's property where appetizers and drinks awaited. There was talk and laughter and the frivolity that accompanies large groups of grandchildren. As we ate and drank, the evening progressed like any other at a family reunion until my grandfather asked us to clear the dance floor; a space that doubled as the cocktail area.

He had brought a portable tape recorder which he cued up with music he brought from home. Stepping aside to give them room, our eyes turned to Bea and Red. But at that moment, they only had eyes for each other. Leading my grandmother by the hand, my grandfather wore a handsome summer suit with a tulip in his lapel. She was dressed in a sunny, yellow pantsuit she'd made herself and a corsage; looking lovely and ready to follow her husband anywhere.

The music started and, like Gene Kelly from a bygone era, my grandfather took my grandmother into his arms and led her the way a man is meant to lead a woman; humbly aware and fully certain that he is nothing without her. And as they danced, everything fell away; all the years full of joy and sadness, all the good and bad they'd encountered. It all vanished, leaving only the two of them; stripped down to nothing but what they meant to each other. Face to face they gazed intently as age and time ceased to matter and the world stood still. Everyone in the room stood silent and watched; honored to be in their presence and grateful to see firsthand what the fruit of fifty years looked like. It was the purest expression of love I'd ever witnessed and I wanted the song to go on and on.

Unfortunately, I soon learned that life doesn't work that way. A year later, the persistent cough we'd all noticed in Vermont turned out to be something more serious. My grandfather had cancer and died just before Thanksgiving in 1982. He was cremated and, instead of a formal funeral, we sat in a circle in the same living room where he played his beloved Dixieland and smoked his cigars, and talked about how much we'd miss him. With one look at my grandmother, I knew she would never get over it. There are some blows in life from which you don't recover. And for that reason, it was the saddest day of my life. She is gone now, too. But when I think of Bea and Red, I picture them on that dance floor; spinning, smiling and deeply in love — forever.

Please turn the page for a preview of . . .

GOLIATH GETS UP

one

"I'm only going to say this once, so listen up. Mark Twain was right. 'There is no God. No universe. No human race. No earthly life. No heaven. No hell. It is all a dream, a grotesque and foolish dream. Nothing exists, but you. And you are but a thought — a vagrant thought, a useless thought, a homeless thought, wandering forlorn among the empty eternities.'"

When teaching tennis to 10-year olds, it is customary to start with the forehand grip, but I was fired last night from the Eggroll Ranch, where I worked part-time as the assistant head cabbage cutter, so I'm feeling angry and unfocused.

"Mister, did you say there's no heaven?"

I memorized Twain's bitter pronouncement at the end of his life for a public speaking class in high school and, unlike most things, it had stayed with me.

"That's right. The whole heaven thing is a big fat lie."

With Mr. Wang's words "you MUSS chop FASSER!"

still ringing in my ears, I find myself face-to-face with seven overindulged fifth-graders ready to break my heart like the rest of the world and its grasping, grabbing inhabitants. Ordinarily, I wouldn't think of letting my new students step between the lines without committing the first three chapters of *The Inner Game of Tennis* to memory, but I've lost heart and with one look I can tell that these three-car garage nambies don't have the moxie to play the sport of kings. They're doomed, dandified muffins; miserably weak and soft, and wholly unfit for mental and physical, mano-a-mano warfare.

"But if there's no heaven, where'd my dog go when he died?"

"Who knows? It's really anybody's guess."

So how did I get such an enormous, throbbing mean-on? It wasn't just my demise as assistant head cabbage cutter, though that was a shock given my contributions to the organization, including a revolutionary expansion of the menu beyond eggrolls. No, like most people, I had a hostility tree with many roots, some deeper than others.

After yesterday's firing, on my birthday no less, despair accompanied me all the way to my girlfriend Miranda's apartment, where I sought a pair of understanding lips and perhaps a Carvel cake, but instead found a pair of men's zebra-print bikini briefs on the stairs leading to her bedroom. Having risked life and limb to reach my beloved by speeding 85 miles-per-hour through a school zone, I was mortified to discover her twisted like a balloon animal around her yoga guru and moaning to the rhythm of a Ravi Shankar sitar medley. Her claim that they were merely trying a back-bending,

Bhagavan Rajneesh prayer position quickly gave way to attempted assault (I took a swing at Casanova with a candlestick) and the sudden departure of Miranda's snake-charming suitor and his stinking exercise mat.

I was devastated. Inside my pocket was a three-quarter carat diamond ring I'd purchased on layaway. I'd finally decided to pop the question and start my life as one half of a legally-recognized, honor-bound institution with all of its rights, responsibilities and semi-regular booty. Unfortunately, I hadn't anticipated someone else's booty getting in the way. Worse yet, Miranda was the sixth woman in a row to leave me for someone else.

"How could you do this?" I asked.

"What's the difference, David? Our relationship is over," Miranda said. "It's been over for awhile."

"Well, this is a hell of a way to let me know. I think I would have preferred an e-mail or a text message."

"It's taken me awhile to figure it out, David, but I finally get it. I finally understand. You are *incapable* of moving your own life forward."

"That's not true."

"You can't hold a job."

"I haven't found the right career," I said.

"You haven't found *any* career. You're all talk. You never follow through on anything."

"So you start sleeping with this guru guy? That's fair."

"I want to be with someone who's going places. And Guru Ganges, for your information, is planning on franchising his yoga studios across the country. You, on the other hand, have no ambition."

"I can't believe you're saying that to me. You work part-time as a cleat specialist at Lady Foot Locker. That doesn't make you Donald Trump in case you're confused. Does someone with no ambition buy the Tony Robbins tapes?"

"That was a year ago, and you've never listened to them."

"It takes time to awaken the giant within. You have to trust me. I've got a long-range plan to improve every aspect of my life."

"Oh, really? Six months ago, you dragged me to that Carlton Sheets no-money-down real estate seminar at the Dome Arena and charged $500 worth of DVDs to my credit card. Have you bid on a single property since then?"

"The market's soft."

"So's your brain. You've let it atrophy. Look at the book you left on my nightstand. *Who Moved My Cheese?* You want to know who moved your cheese? Nobody. You don't have any cheese to move."

"Maybe not, but I've got five of the seven habits of highly effective people. Two more and I'm golden. *We're* golden."

"I'm not buying it anymore, David. Face it — you're a loser and you'll always be a loser."

Try as I might to teach these ghastly kids standing in front of me now, I couldn't shake Miranda's parting words. By her estimation, I had numerous deep-seated Freudian and ESPN-related issues. In attacking me, she employed hurtful adjectives including insensitive, lazy, emotionally distant and poorly dressed, and said she'd moved beyond me with the Chakra breath work and brain respiration techniques she learned from her yogi. She even had the nerve to tell me that I was spiritually bankrupt while she stumbled around looking for her Wonderbra.

I couldn't see it then but Miranda isn't anything special. She's kind of plain and pudgy; not particularly bright or charming or accomplished. She isn't a woman of incomparable grace or unending patience and, on a scale of one to ten, I'd rate her compassion for pets and old people a three. She just turned 30, the age at which some women panic about being unmarried and begin hunting for a mate with a single-minded ruthlessness. Yet, here I'd been on the verge of doing something that countless men and women do every year — marry the wrong person. Why does this happen? It's complicated, isn't it? For me, the answer resided in my subconscious. I didn't think a bumbler with ebbing testosterone, non-existent job prospects and thirty-four dollars in his checking account deserved better. My disregard for myself, my fear of being alone and my growing sense of mortality were pushing me toward the precipice like an aging convertible being driven by Thelma and Louise.

In my weakest moment, I listed Miranda's positives and negatives on a piece of paper; desperately trying to quantify her; hoping to find some equation that would convince me of the things I didn't feel in my heart. If this is your preferred method of deciding yes or no on a potential mate, the answer is always no. To let your marital choice become a gradual acquiescence due to pressure, fatigue and a ticking clock rather than an affirmative act powered by illogical inspiration is a mistake.

For months, Miranda had continually talked about rings, china patterns and girlfriends who were getting married, setting up house, having children and moving on with their lives. All the talk, however, was less about me than it was about the deeds; about the need to check these items off some list that would make her complete in the eyes of others. What changed was she found a better prospect.

In retrospect, I admit that ramming her pre-owned Nissan Altima with my '75 Ford Mustang (pumpkin-colored with an odometer stuck at 368,312 miles) was a bit rash, but after explaining that "Gigi" was a curry-flavored freak who satisfied her sexually in ways I never could, Miranda kicked me out of her house. Understandably, this threw me into the type of vengeance spiral I was warned about previously by Judge Stander, a local mediator and hostage negotiator, following an unfortunate incident involving my favorite shirt and a local dry-cleaner.

One piece of advice: never give the woman you love a gift certificate for 24 sessions at the Indo-Aryan Yoga Shack. Now, besides my twice-weekly tennis gig, all I had in life was a part-time job selling slightly-used Tibetan prayer rugs at Who's Your Llama?, an upscale boutique catering to mooks who say things like, "I'm bringing my iPad to base camp so I can blog." With neither love nor meaningful work to speak of, I took some small comfort in warning my students about life's predators.

"Don't wait. Start your enemies list today," I said.

"What's an enemies list?"

Danny Cohen, a four foot three inch student with a yarmulke pinned to his head and a massive Prince racket in his right hand, was momentarily intrigued. Nixonian paranoia may be unbecoming but, after last night, I realize I should have started scrawling down the names of the awful people who mean me harm much, much sooner.

"It's a record of every subhuman cretin draining the marrow from your bones. Start with your ex-girlfriend's yoga instructor, then add every boss who's ever fired you, particularly ones with cabbage fetishes from

GOLIATH GETS UP 7

cowboy-themed, eggroll eateries located in strip malls."

"I don't get it."

Danny and the rest of the class looked confused.

"Let me try again. It's a list of every bloodsucker plotting your downfall."

Danny never heard straight talk like that. Not even in temple. He pondered my words for a moment before losing interest. He was, after all, only 10.

"Are you a pirate?" Danny asked.

"No, I'm not a pirate. Do you see a parrot on my shoulder?"

"Why do you wear that eye patch?"

"Mind your own business, okay?"

"Why are your shorts so short? They look gay."

This insensitive question came from Willa Nash, the only 165 lb. fifth grader I knew with a monogrammed water bottle, invariably filled with Pimp Juice, an energy drink for malcontents and their snowboarding instructors. By failing to demand a more respectful tongue from their tomboy daughter, Willa's father, Kit, and her absentee mother, Missy, an area veterinarian/plastic surgeon specializing in extreme makeovers of pets and their owners, had loosed yet one more monster on society.

"There is nothing *gay* about these shorts. They're timeless, both in fit and style," I said.

"Timeless, my butt."

"Stifle it, Willa, or I'll drop you like a bag of mulch!"

If this girl, with her low-hanging Bermudas, "Skate or Die" T-shirt, and maddening 'tude, continued her line of questioning, she would soon find her name added to the list of those I would lay to waste. My shorts, which covered the uppermost portion of my thighs at rest and much less upon flight, admittedly challenged most public decency laws, clinging to my rear end like Saran Wrap stuck to a Mylar balloon. But there was a perfectly good reason why I wouldn't abandon them or my shirts, relics from the Ivan Lendl collection, complete with tattered necks and yellowed underarms: I didn't have the disposable income to buy a Blizzard at Dairy Queen let alone a new tennis ensemble.

On most days, my money woes sufficed as a valid justification for my current mental condition and freed me to ponder more pressing concerns like who to vote for on *American Idol* or which whitening toothpaste I needed. Unfortunately, my prior evening's disappointments (e.g. the Eggroll Ranch and Miranda) coupled with the incessant prattling of Willa, the poster girl for childhood obesity, forced me to confront a second, less practical but more honest reason why I wore my old athletic clothes.

The truth was that these aging tennis outfits reminded me of who I'd been at one time during a period in my life when anything seemed possible and stitched to the sleeve of each of my shirts and every pair of shorts was a symbol of strength adorned by my mother.

"What's that stupid lizard on your shorts?" Willa asked.

"It's not a stupid lizard. It's a dragon," I said.

"Well, it looks gay. Are we gonna play tennis or what?"

"Watch your tone, Calamity Jane. And put down the Pimp Juice."

I never knew that "gay" was such a popular word with ten-year olds, but Willa used it more often than an Oscar Wilde scholar discussing his Keith Haring collection.

"Why do you have a dragon on your shorts?" Danny Cohen asked, suddenly interested again.

"It's a long story so never mind. Everybody shake hands with their racket," I said.

I held out my Wilson T-2000, perpendicular to the ground, and demonstrated the Eastern forehand grip. "Today, we're going to learn how to hit a forehand."

"David, am I doing it right?"

"Let me see, Becky."

I pulled my smallest student, Becky Pardi, clad in a pinafore and wearing pigtails, away from the procession of Violet Beauregardes and Augustus Gloops lining up to take their turns on the ball machine. Becky held out her racket to show me her grip.

"Turn your hand a bit to the right," I said.

"Like this?" Becky asked.

"That's it. You've got it. Now try again."

Trying again. Getting the right grip. Actions easier said than done and increasingly improbable in my mind as I assessed my life less than twelve months from my fortieth birthday. Someone once said that 40 is when your life comes together and your body falls apart, but in my case, both were falling apart. Ten years ago, I'd never experienced the joys of lower back pain, acute shoulder bursitis or overgrown nose hair. Today, they were welcome distractions from my plantar fasciitis and sore Achilles that made standing for hours on a tennis court a curse.

"Huddle up, group. We're almost out of time . . . Listen, I owe you guys an apology."

To these imps and the rest of the world, I am David Horvath, part-time teaching pro, late night cabbage cutter and frequent wearer of unmentionable atrocities. But years ago, when I took lessons for everything from tennis to chess to tae kwon do, and competed in spelling bees, soap box derbies and ski races, I went by the name of Dragon, a nickname my mother gave to me for reasons that remain unclear. It may have been just a clever device she used to change my self-perception after I was diagnosed at age two with a degenerative condition in my cornea that caused intense light sensitivity and required me to keep my right eye covered at all times with a patch. More likely, she knew that the absence of my father, and my growing awareness of its significance, created a void in my life and necessitated assurance that I was not merely okay but, rather, indomitable.

Whatever the case, the name change worked for awhile as my mother bolstered my confidence by extolling the virtues of these scaly beasts and, by association, me. According to her, I was going to be great and the records of history, as well as the scrap books she purchased at Woolworth's for $4.99 a piece, were waiting to be filled with pictures and tales of my future achievements. I imagine she thought I would scale Everest, win an Oscar, advise presidents and inspire a dance craze. I would sing at Carnegie Hall, collect gold at the Olympics, marry a princess and end world hunger. No accomplishment was beyond my reach, and the mark I'd leave on this world would be lasting and large. Mind you none of this jibed with the team of specialists trying to teach me to read at school, but this was my mother talking and who was I to disagree? If I hadn't been petrified of heights, I would've grabbed a red cape and jumped off the roof of our house.

My mother was a strong believer in self-fulfilling prophecies and once she started sewing dragons on every pair of Toughskins and second-hand Lacoste shirts I owned (replacing the crocodile), the idea that I would rise to the level of her expectations became less far-fetched. The yellow, red and green threads embedded in my clothes infused me with energy; the tight stitching holding me and my fragile psyche together. I wore my dragons the way a Marine wears his patches — *Semper Fi*. I was an army of one plus one, my mom, who, in addition to using needle and thread, wielded a paint brush to put a fire-breathing hydra with a pair of flaming nostrils on just about everything I owned from the banana seat on my bike to my skateboard to my bedroom wall, all in an attempt to spur me on to the summit. Her technique would have made for a wonderful article in the kind of hyper-parenting magazines you see today, squeezed somewhere between anxiety-provoking pieces about 529 college plans and Sudden Infant Death Syndrome, if not for one fatal flaw: I stunk at everything.

Now, before you think I'm being too hard on myself, let me clarify. When it came to receiving athletic instruction, I was an above-average, some would say highly proficient, listener, but my lack of depth perception prevented me from converting words into deeds and soon I had one of the largest private collections of light blue honorable mention ribbons and certificates of participation on the East coast. If a major league scout from any sport had been watching me, his critique would have read, 'too slow, too short, too weak, but gives it holy hell.' Indeed, nobody tried harder than me, but effort only takes you so far when you're throwing up on the coach after each set of wind-sprints and sweating through your eye patch.

Baseball proved particularly challenging though

no sport came easily. Mr. Saunders, my little league manager, who had one tooth, no conscience and a pronounced limp from "killin' a man" in self-defense according to local lore, instructed me to start a fight every time we got behind by spitting a wad of chewing tobacco into the opposing team's dugout or kicking their coach in the nuts. As I recall, we were the only team whose skipper provided each player with sharpened, steel-tipped cleats and a tin of Skoal before all games. Mostly I remember right field in the hot summer and the staring contests I'd enter with random dandelions. Standing firmly in the ready position during my league-mandated two innings, I kept waiting for my volcano of baseball heroism to erupt at any moment, but it never did. All my dreams of hitting a home run over the centerfield fence at Bob Ford Field remained buried in the soil of some Mudville Nine nightmare scenario of strikeouts and weak, Texas-league singles struggling mightily to make it over the first baseman's head.

My mother, who loved Louis Armstrong, thought cornet might be my calling and bought me a beautiful vintage brass instrument from a yard sale. My music teacher, Miss Lovell, wasn't as enthusiastic informing her soon thereafter that I was tone deaf and rhythmically-challenged unlike any other student she'd been affiliated with while suggesting that I give up the pursuit. I can still hear my mother arguing my case until Miss Lovell, in a fit of frustration, said that Stevie Wonder could read music better than me.

When I moved on to the dramatic arts, things looked promising initially as I landed the role of munchkin number 27 in the junior high school production of

The Wizard of Oz. After explaining that it was a non-speaking part, Mr. Denison, the drama coach, told me to hide behind a crudely-constructed wooden bush for the entire play, sapping my enthusiasm for acting and, for that matter, set design. Nevertheless, despite the disappointments, I was continually assured by my mother that my time was coming and that these were minor setbacks on the way to major victories.

Athletic, musical and dramatic mediocrity wouldn't have been so bad, but I wasn't much of a wiz in the classroom either. In the sixth grade city-wide spelling bee, I forgot the first 'e' in 'excellent' causing a collective groan in the audience so loud, it's still remembered vividly by event organizers to this day. No matter how much my mother helped me with homework, quizzed me with flash cards or promised me cash, I always came home with a report card full of C's and D's. Notably missing were any remarks about not working up to potential. I wasn't dumb, but my loose grip on phonics put me at a disadvantage when compared to my classmates.

Through it all, Peggy, as my mother was known to the women she worked with at Betty's Beauty Nook, continually tried to help me in ways both obvious and subtle. Among other things, I give her credit for never bad-mouthing my biological father. Instead of trying to convince me that he was a bastard who'd screwed us over, she insisted that he was a handsome, smart, funny man who left with her blessing and loved me though we'd never met. Year after year, she kept the details of his whereabouts sketchy, insinuating that he was off on a quixotic journey far, far away, fighting the forces of evil. And notwithstanding my hurtful discovery that

Han Solo was not my dad after three years of insisting everyone call me Chewbacca, I intuitively understood and appreciated my mother's efforts to mythologize this man in order to protect me.

At night, sitting on the edge of my bed made up with NFL sheets, her head eclipsing the hallway light, my mother led us in the Lord's Prayer, read me a poem from her Norton Anthology, and then told me tales about dragons. According to her, ancient civilizations from the Sumerians to the Babylonians to the Aztecs feared dragons as evil, but the Chinese saw them as emblematic of everything good and called themselves Lung Tik Chuan Ren, descendants of dragons. To them, dragons brought abundance, prosperity and good fortune, and were courageous, wise, strong, heroic, perseverant and noble — all the things I was going to be. My mother *insisted* that I, too, was a descendant of Chinese dragons and a celestial creature who would overcome all obstacles in my path on the way to greatness. And though she never focused precisely on how I would become dragon-great as opposed to the slightly above-average yet content person I'd originally envisioned, she insisted my greatness was inherent, pre-destined and waiting to emerge, a theory as water-tight as an Indonesian ferryboat, but one I bought and gladly climbed aboard.

Growing up, I constantly looked to my mother for assurance about my direction and prospects and then, without warning, everything changed when I was nineteen. She died on a Saturday and, immediately, the robust force at my back disappeared and my forward momentum slowed. Soon, thereafter, I stalled out. More than 20 years later I'm stuck, and lately I'm gripped, unlike ever before, by the type of fear that paralyzes a man for whom greatness is predicted, but not yet achieved: the fear of leaving this world without a legacy. Halfway through life, I'm still waiting for the moment to arrive when the promise of the past will be realized and, for the first time, wondering whether my mother was wrong. To wake up one morning and find yourself to be ordinary and average, entirely unremarkable, is easier for those of whom little is hoped. But for those who have feasted on a diet of expectations, it is a staggering blow followed by a creeping sense of dread and moments of panic. Did dragons exist or was I just a mythical beast conjured up for the sake of my self-esteem? Had my mother simply soothed my childhood wounds with her stories or did she know something about me that would yet be revealed?

The answer would seem obvious. Anthropologists agree that dragons never existed. According to these experts, they have always been a mere figment of imagination — a mental morphing of the most feared animals in the Earth's history. Given this fact, maybe I should relegate the winged dragon to the dim place where Santa Claus and the Easter Bunny reside after children no longer believe. After all, overwhelming odds say the experts are right. Plus, I'm not stupid. I can look in a mirror and see that I bear no resemblance to anything other than what I am: a 39-year old, emotionally arrested man clinging to his youth the way a white-knuckle flyer clings to his armrest during severe turbulence. I'm not green. I have no scales or tail. And, except for a brief bout of madness last summer involving grain alcohol and a Bic lighter, I have no ability to spit fire.

STARBUCK O'DWYER

Am I a dragon? Is it possible that I'm the latest incarnation of a beast that came before me, imbued with all the characteristics of such a creature as my mother described them? Am I a living heir, like the Lung Tik Chuan Ren? I don't know. What I do know is that I must embrace the dragon dream that something better, some kind of greatness, exists within me just waiting to ignite like flames from the nose of an ancient green monster. I can no longer rely solely on cosmic forces unknown to sweep me up and deliver me to my rightful place and destiny. Instead, I need to act in concert with these forces, consciously reinventing myself, in order to have any chance at something resembling a life; and I need to do it by the time I turn 40.